Collins Revised

# Engaging English 6

## Workbook

Anju Gupta

# Components of DigiSuite

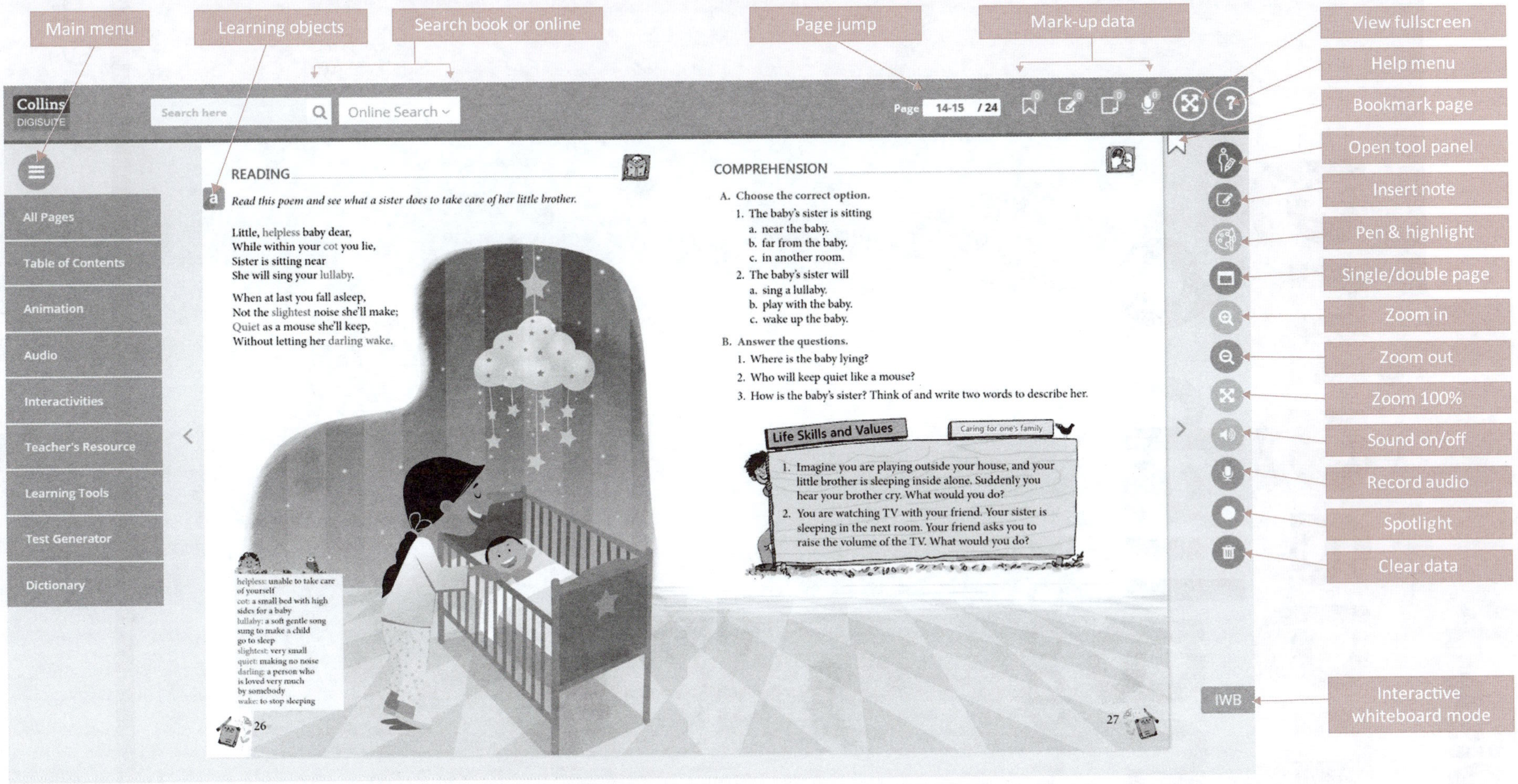


## Student + Teacher

**a** animations

**ilt** instructor-led tutorials

**ia** activities

**w** worksheets

audio

**g** games

**v** videos

## Teacher-only

**lp** lesson plans

**w** worksheets

**tn** teacher's notes

**ak** answer keys

# Preface

***Revised Engaging English*** aims to instill an appreciation for literature in today's learners, while equipping them with the tools to develop native fluency and communicative competence in using the English language. The eight-level series comprises Coursebooks, Workbooks, and digital resources for teachers for all levels.

The revised edition has been aligned closely with the guidelines of the National Education Policy, 2020 through its focus on twenty-first century skills, Sustainable Development Goals (SDGs), cross-curricular learning, 'Happiness' content and art-integrated learning. Coursebooks and Workbooks 1 and 2 integrate the essence of NIPUN (National Initiative for Proficiency in Reading with Understanding and Numeracy). They aim to motivate students to read independently, improve their vocabulary, develop their critical thinking and creative skills and enhance their ability to express themselves verbally and in writing.

The lessons are built around carefully selected literary pieces with distinct cross-curricular themes, and presented with glossary, explanation of literary terms and interesting trivia. The end-of-chapter exercises address the needs of formal language learning.

The **Workbooks** are designed to complement the Coursebooks, by providing additional skills practice, review and assessments. They comprise the following sections:

**Comprehension** includes factual, inferential and evaluative questions based on short reading passages.

**Way with Words** includes exercises on the vocabulary topics encountered in the Coursebook as well as extension activities derived from it. It also incorporates activities on literary devices and figures of speech, spelling drills and exercises on dictionary usage.

**Grammar in Use** starts with a short explanation of important grammar concepts covered in the Coursebook, followed by plenty of practice for reinforcement.

**Listening and Speaking** builds students' oral and aural communication skills. It includes tasks such as phonics drills, conversation practice, role plays and debates to develop spoken English skills. Listening comprehension exercises teach students to listen for both general and specific details. In poetry chapters, there are activities on stress, rhyme and metre.

**Pen it Down:** The activities in this section include guided and free writing tasks derived from the reading text, which build on the functional and creative writing skills of the learner.

Each Workbook also contains two **Tests**. One of these is based on the principle of SAFAL (Structured Assessment For Analyzing Learning), a competency-based assessment introduced by CBSE. They assess the competencies of critical thinking as well as inquiry-based and analysis-based learning. The other test is modelled on class assessments.

The series encourages competency-based education which allows concept acquisition at the learner's own pace, based on individual ability. We hope that it will foster a love for literature and reading in young learners.

# Detailed Contents

| Unit | Theme | Way with Words | Grammar in Use | Listening and Speaking | Pen it Down |
|---|---|---|---|---|---|
| 10. I am Malala | Education of the Girl Child | • Homonyms and homophones | • Prepositions<br>• Inappropriate shift in tenses | • Listening to an extract from a book and answering questions | • Essay writing about a cause |
| 11. The Nightingale | Music and Creativity | • Antonyms<br>• Sounds related to birds | • Simple and continuous tenses | • Proverbs and their meanings | • Essay writing |
| 12. The Tale of Custard the Dragon | Humour | • Metaphors<br>• Onomatopoeic words<br>• Words with similar meanings | • Phrases and clauses<br>• Main and subordinate clauses | • Pair work: narrating an incident | • Picture composition |
| 13. Bruno Goes Exploring | War and Peace | • Commonly confused words<br>• Collocations | • Nouns: abstract and compound<br>• Tenses: perfect and perfect continuous | • Conversation: introducing someone and speaking about him/her | • Paragraph writing |
| 14. Building a Windmill | Science and Technology | • Contextual usage<br>• Words related to professions | • Active and passive voice<br>• Coordinating conjunctions | • Pair work: show and tell activity on how objects are made | • Report writing |
| 15. Peter of Haarlem | Brave Deeds | • Idioms: related to body parts; related to work and business<br>• Words used as nouns and verbs | • Reflexive and indefinite pronouns<br>• Types of phrases | • Conversation: speaking about a person | • Second-person account |
| 16. A Visit from St Nicholas | Celebrations | • Words related to Christmas | • Demonstrative and interrogative pronouns<br>• Subordinating and correlative conjunctions | • Forming questions for given answers | • Diary entry<br>• Descriptive account |
| 17. In the Rue Bel Tesoro - I | Hard Times | • Phrasal verbs with *play*<br>• Words related to emotions | • Direct and indirect speech | • Conversation: speaking on a given topic | • Writing a travelogue<br>• Formal letter |
| 18. In the Rue Bel Tesoro - II | Hard Times | • Adjectives<br>• Using *farther* and *further* | • Types of sentences: simple, compound and complex | • Conversation: responding to questions | • Writing a play |
| **Assessment (SAFAL)** | | | | | |

# Contents

# 1

Our Country

# The Questions

## Comprehension

**Read the passage and answer the questions.**

Severe storms are caused by low-pressure weather systems. As warm, wet air begins to rise, it becomes cooler. Water vapour in the air turns into water droplets by a process called condensation. These droplets join together to form clouds, and then precipitation in some form (rain, sleet, snow or hail) falls down on to the Earth's surface.

Thunderstorms represent the most common kind of extreme weather. Before a thunderstorm can develop, three conditions have to be present: the air has to be full of moisture, there must be either an intensely heated portion of the Earth's surface sending warm air up quickly or an approaching cold front (the edge of a cooler mass of air near the Earth's surface), and lastly, the warm air that is rising from the Earth must be warmer than the air it passes through as it rises.

The moisture in the rising air condenses, clouds form and a storm begins. A cold front occurs when cold air moves near the Earth's surface and pushes warm air up very quickly. This is often the beginning of a thunderstorm. Clouds form, and rain starts falling heavily. Opposite electrical charges inside storm clouds separate, causing lightning to flash. Lightning has enough energy to heat the air all around it. This sudden burst of heat causes the noise that we hear as thunder. Thunderstorms often bring disasters with them, including floods, fires caused by lightning, damage from hailstones or strong winds, and even tornadoes. A tornado is a spinning mass of air over land that can destroy almost everything in its path.

A blizzard is a combination of strong winds and low temperatures. In a blizzard, snowfall increases until it is so heavy that it is difficult or impossible to see. People can get lost in the snow and freeze to death. Homes can be enveloped in snow, trapping people indoors.

A hurricane is the most powerful form of thunderstorms. Forming over warm ocean waters off the coast of the tropics, hurricanes can become gigantic swirling mixtures of air and water between 100 and 900 miles wide. Wind speeds can average about 75 miles per hour. Hurricanes mostly damage coastal cities because they quickly lose their strength when they move over land. Hurricanes are so large and powerful that their swirling clouds can even be seen from space.

**A. Choose the correct options to complete the sentences.**

1. Water vapour in the air forms droplets by a process called ____________.

   a. evaporation b. condensation c. precipitation

2. ____________ is a kind of precipitation.

   a. Air b. Sleet c. Lightning

3. Clouds are formed due to the ________.
   a. collection of dust   b. cooling of moisture in the air   c. swirling mixtures of air
4. A ________ is the most powerful form of thunderstorms.
   a. blizzard   b. tornado   c. hurricane
5. Hurricanes are so large and powerful that their swirling clouds can be seen from ________.
   a. homes   b. space   c. a distance

**B. Answer the questions in a few lines.**

1. What are the three conditions that must exist for the development of a thunderstorm?
2. Describe a hurricane.
3. How are lightning and thunder caused?
4. Name the types of disasters thunderstorms can cause.
5. Compare a tornado and a blizzard.

## Way with Words

### Antonyms

**A. State whether the word pairs are antonyms (A) or synonyms (S).**

| | | | |
|---|---|---|---|
| 1. big, minuscule | ________ | 6. fantastic, wonderful | ________ |
| 2. amazing, awesome | ________ | 7. cheap, inexpensive | ________ |
| 3. huge, vast | ________ | 8. dear, costly | ________ |
| 4. lustre, brilliance | ________ | 9. unimpressive, ordinary | ________ |
| 5. awful, wonderful | ________ | 10. simple, elaborate | ________ |

B. **Match the words in column A with their antonyms in column B.**

| A | B |
|---|---|
| 1. separate | a. contraction |
| 2. boring | b. detached |
| 3. expansion | c. infinite |
| 4. innovative | d. determined |
| 5. connected | e. exciting |
| 6. dead | f. dull |
| 7. finite | g. ambitious |
| 8. indecisive | h. quarrelsome |
| 9. unmotivated | i. connect |
| 10. amiable | j. alive |

## Grammar in Use

### Types of Adverbs

You know that adverbs modify verbs, and even adjectives and other adverbs.

**Examples:**
Birbal spoke to Akbar **patiently** → The highlighted word is an **adverb of manner**.
The sheep were brought **inside**. → The highlighted word is an **adverb of place**.
The emperor and the courtiers met **later**. → The highlighted word is an **adverb of time**.
Birbal answered the courtiers' questions **regularly**. → The highlighted word is an **adverb of frequency**.

A. **Identify the type of adverb in each sentence and rewrite it correctly.**

1. I nearby live.

______________________________________

______________________________________

2. I hardly nowadays listen to music.

______________________________________

______________________________________

3. Your order tomorrow shall arrive.

______________________________________

______________________________________

4. Sunny crept silently up on his brother.

______________________________________

______________________________________

5. I sincerely worked on the project.

_______________________________________________

6. I'm going to school back.

_______________________________________________

7. I called immediately the plumber.

_______________________________________________

8. He went and bought the car ahead.

_______________________________________________

**B. Find the adjective in the first sentence. Complete the second sentence using the adverb formed from that adjective.**

1. Jatin is angry. He is speaking ______________.
2. The music is loud. It is playing ______________.
3. Her French is fluent. She speaks French ______________.
4. My uncle is a careless driver. He drives ______________.
5. The actor is good. He acts ______________.
6. My neighbour is a wonderful cook. She cooks ______________.
7. The girl is a very graceful dancer. She dances ______________.
8. This exercise is simple. You ______________ have to fill in the blanks with adverbs.
9. The soldiers are brave. They fought ______________.

## Question Tags

A **question tag** is the short question at the end of a statement.

**Example:** Birbal is intelligent, **isn't he**?

**C. Complete the sentences with the correct question tags.**

1. The new boy is from Italy, ______________?
2. The baby isn't sleeping, ______________?
3. You are the new gardener, ______________?
4. She went to the market yesterday, ______________?
5. He didn't like the pasta, ______________?
6. Cars pollute the environment, ______________?
7. An apple a day keeps the doctor away, ______________?
8. The new car was very expensive, ______________?
9. It is wrong to tell a lie, ______________?
10. The English teacher explains the text well, ______________?

## Listening and Speaking

**Listen to some facts about Akbar and Birbal. Then answer the questions.**

1. Who were the Navaratnas?
2. Why was Birbal a close friend of Akbar's?
3. Who was the treasurer in the Mughal court?
4. What was Birbal's role in the court?
5. What was the period of Akbar's rule?

## Pen it Down

**Imagine you were in Mumbai visiting your cousins, when Cyclone Tauktae hit Maharashtra. Mumbai was also affected by it. This was your first experience of facing an extreme weather condition. Write a diary entry expressing your feelings.**

You can include the following points in your diary entry:

- Describe the situation and what you saw
- Mention what safety measures were taken by your cousins and you
- Write how the experience affected you

# 2
# Voyage

## Way with Words

### Similes

**A. Match the similes with their meanings.**

| Similes | Meanings |
|---|---|
| 1. as large as life | a. understand something clearly |
| 2. busy as a bee | b. be in a good condition |
| 3. run like the wind | c. fight bravely |
| 4. slither like a snake | d. cry a lot without any reason |
| 5. clear as crystal | e. be very big and important |
| 6. proud as a peacock | f. be very smart |
| 7. as good as gold | g. be very busy |
| 8. as bright as a button | h. move quickly and quietly |
| 9. fight like a lion | i. run fast |
| 10. cry like a baby | j. be extremely proud |

### Idiomatic Expressions

**B. Tick the option that best explains the meaning of each idiom given in bold.**

1. Ravi wanted to impress his uncle. So he **bent over backwards** to look after him.
   a. Ravi did very little to impress his uncle. ☐
   b. Ravi tried very hard to impress his uncle. ☐
2. The children would have kept playing **until the cows came home** if their parents had not called them in to do their homework.
   a. The children were waiting for the cows to come back. ☐
   b. The children would have continued playing till it was dark. ☐

3. Atul's father buys him expensive presents **at the drop of a hat**.

   a. Atul's father buys gifts for him very often.

   b. Atul's father drops a hat whenever he buys a present for him.

4. It was difficult for the children to keep **a stiff upper lip** when their pet dog died.

   a. The children had difficulty in keeping their lips in proper shape.

   b. It was difficult for the children not to cry when their pet dog died.

5. Ruby was excited about learning French, but after the first class she was ready to **jump ship**.

   a. Ruby wanted to stop learning French.

   b. Ruby wanted to jump from a ship in excitement.

6. The new boss looked very strict, but the subordinates soon found that her **bark was worse than her bite**.

   a. The new boss has a dog who barks and bites.

   b. The new boss looks stricter than she actually is.

## Grammar in Use

### Auxiliary Verbs

You know that auxiliary verbs are used with the main verbs to convey the tense or mood of the main verbs.

Primary auxiliary verbs are **be**, **do** and **have**.

**Examples:** She **is** reading a book. (be)

Father **did** look tired. (do)

The teacher **had** asked her to speak loudly. (have)

**Modals** are also auxiliary verbs. They include **can** and **could** (ability and permission), **will** and **would** (wish, prediction, request or demand), **shall** (determination, purpose), **should** (request or offer), **may** and **might** (possibility and permission), **must** (strong belief or possibility) and **ought** (suggestion).

**Complete the sentences with the correct auxiliary verbs.**

1. What ____________ you done to the vase? It is broken!

   a. were  b. did  c. have

2. I ____________ not going to school today. I am feeling unwell.

   a. am  b. were  c. did

3. My best friend from Mumbai ____________ sent me a gift.

   a. did  b. has  c. is

4. I __________ not need to go to school today as it is a holiday.
   a. do  b. have  c. is

5. I __________ really enjoying my piano lessons.
   a. am  b. are  c. is

6. __________ you watch the cricket match last night?
   a. Have  b. Did  c. Are

7. __________ this zoo have a bear?
   a. Has  b. Does  c. Is

8. __________ you ever eaten spaghetti?
   a. Is  b. Have  c. Did

9. Her train __________ just arrived.
   a. has  b. does  c. is

10. __________ you know the way to the market?
   a. Have  b. Do  c. Are

## Listening and Speaking

**Divide the class into pairs. The partners will narrate the details of a voyage to a magical land from their imagination. The other partner will then ask them questions, such as:**

- What was your favourite part of the journey?
- What kind of magical creatures did you meet along the way?
- What difficulties did you face on the voyage?
- Can you share any other details about the voyage?

**The students will listen carefully to each other's answers and then introduce their partner to the class and tell the class about their partner's magical voyage.**

## Pen it Down

**You have recently been on an eventful trip to the mountains with your parents and siblings. Write a letter to your friend about your trip. You can talk about these points in your letter:**

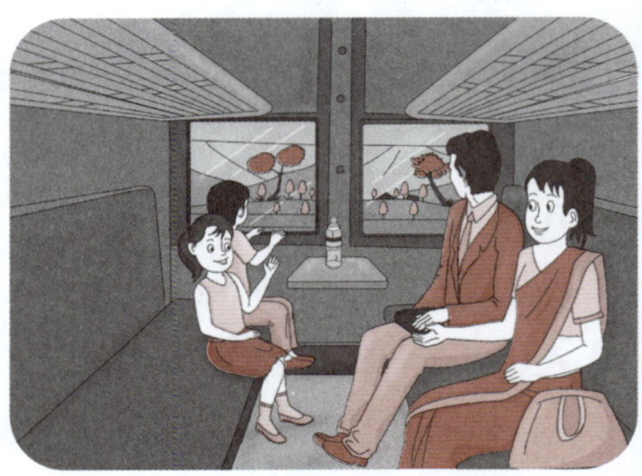

- describe the place you visited, the weather and the scenery
- the things you did while on the trip
- the local food you ate, and the people you met
- add idioms and similes to your descriptions

# 3

Crime and Detection

# Peril at End House

## Way with Words

### Mystery Words

**A. Spot fifteen mystery words hidden in the grid.**

| T | A | E | V | I | D | E | N | C | E | W | Q |
|---|---|---|---|---|---|---|---|---|---|---|---|
| P | A | L | I | B | I | B | T | Q | G | S | K |
| U | C | O | N | M | X | T | M | H | A | L | P |
| Z | Z | J | G | O | L | W | H | U | F | E | C |
| Z | N | R | X | T | J | I | T | N | T | U | R |
| L | S | S | D | I | C | T | M | C | I | T | I |
| E | E | U | K | V | X | N | K | H | K | H | M |
| S | T | S | D | E | T | E | C | T | I | V | E |
| S | T | P | W | O | T | S | W | A | P | C | P |
| T | I | E | E | F | D | S | R | U | B | L | L |
| J | N | C | M | Y | S | T | E | R | Y | U | O |
| H | G | T | V | I | C | T | I | M | L | E | T |

### Contextual Usage

**B. Write sentences with these words and phrases from the story.**

1. be a thrill ______
2. to your good health ______
3. by pure chance ______
4. impressed upon ______
5. tamper with ______

## Grammar in Use

### Subject, Verb and Object

The **subject** in a sentence is the doer of the action. The **verb** denotes the action in a sentence. The **object** is the part of a sentence that is acted on or the verb is directed towards.

**Example:** Poirot took the glass. (subject: Poirot; verb: took; object: glass)

**A. Identify the subject, the verb and the direct object for each sentence.**

1. She visits her grandparents every summer.
   subject: ___________; verb or verb phrase: ___________; direct object: ___________
2. Swimming in the sea for too long might be harmful for the skin.
   subject: ___________; verb or verb phrase: ___________; direct object: ___________
3. The parents read stories to the child at night.
   subject: ___________; verb or verb phrase: ___________; direct object: ___________
4. Mona was not able to play because of her broken arm.
   subject: ___________; verb or verb phrase: ___________; direct object: ___________
5. A bee flying in the garden sat on the roses.
   subject: ___________; verb or verb phrase: ___________; direct object: ___________
6. My friend is playing the guitar in the school concert.
   subject: ___________; verb or verb phrase: ___________; direct object: ___________
7. Our neighbours bought a new car.
   subject: ___________; verb or verb phrase: ___________; direct object: ___________
8. Walking in the morning is good for health.
   subject: ___________; verb or verb phrase: ___________; direct object: ___________
9. The rush hour traffic causes many office goers to get delayed.
   subject: ___________; verb or verb phrase: ___________; direct object: ___________
10. Soham wanted to pursue a career in finance and so he studied accounting.
    subject: ___________; verb or verb phrase: ___________; direct object: ___________

### Agreement of the Subject and Verb

Agreement of the subject and verb refers to the relationship between the subject and predicate of a sentence. Subjects and verbs in sentences must always agree in tense and number.

**Examples:** **Poirot** solves crimes using his intelligence. (both the subject **Poirot** and the verb *solves* are singular)

**Bees** collect nectar from flowers. (both the subject **Bees** and the verb *collect* are plural)

**B. Choose the correct form of the verb so that it agrees with the subject in each sentence.**

1. Anjana and her friends (is/are) playing.
2. Either my mother or my father (is/are) coming to the school sports day.
3. The dog and its pups (is/are) outside.
4. Either my sister or your brother (is/are) always troubling us during games.
5. Mother and father (doesn't/don't) want to eat Chinese food today.
6. She (doesn't/don't) know the answer.
7. One of my classmates (is/are) going on a trip to France.
8. The man with all the parrots (live/lives) on my street.
9. The players, as well as the captain, (want/wants) to win.
10. Mathematics (is/are) my favourite subject.

### Subject-Verb Agreement with Intervening Phrases and Clauses

In a sentence, intervening phrases and clauses may separate the subject and the verb. In such sentences, we should identify the subject and the verb to ensure that they agree with each other.

**Examples:** The **detectives** in the room are talking to Nick. (intervening phrase: in the room)

**Mott**, disappointed with the mechanic's work, fired him the next day. (intervening clause: disappointed with the mechanic's work)

**C. Rewrite the sentences with correct subject-verb agreement.**

1. The museum, located in the middle of the city, have many artifacts and antique paintings.

   ________________________________________

   ________________________________________

2. Do the restaurant, which opened near our house recently, serve Thai food?

   ________________________________________

   ________________________________________

3. The students, excited about the trip, was making a lot of noise.

   ________________________________________

   ________________________________________

4. Each of the criminals involved in the armed robbery were arrested.

   ________________________________________

   ________________________________________

5. Many of the apples, which we bought yesterday, was rotten.

   ________________________________________

   ________________________________________

6. The Indian athletes, who participated in the Tokyo 2020 Olympics, has performed exceptionally well.

______________________________________________

______________________________________________

## Listening and Speaking

You learnt about silent letters in the coursebook.
**Example:** Poirot (**t** is silent)

**A. Say these words aloud and underline the silent letter in each word.**

| | | | |
|---|---|---|---|
| debt | honest | watch | wrench |
| knife | boulder | plumber | knob |

**B. Take turns to answer some questions about mystery books. The questions will be asked by your classmates. While one student is answering the questions, the rest of the class will listen to the answers.**

You may ask the following questions:

1. Have you read any mystery book?
2. What do you think a mystery is?
3. When you hear the word 'mystery', what comes to your mind first?
4. Which is your favourite mystery book, movie or TV programme?
5. Do you feel scared when watching a mystery show/movie?
6. What do you think makes a good mystery?

**You can also form your own questions and ask them.**

## Pen it Down

The purpose of a notice is to announce or display information to a particular group of people. Notices are usually put up in public spaces prominently so people can view them easily.

**You are the student editor of your school magazine and want to publish a special edition to celebrate Hercule Poirot's birthday on July 17. Write a notice in not more than 50 words inviting entries on this theme for the special issue of the magazine.**

You can mention the following details:

- what entries can be sent: articles, stories, cartoons, poems and fact sheets

- maximum number of words allowed, format (handwritten, printed, email) and where to submit
- themes to explore, such as Poirot's greatest mysteries, real-life inspiration...
- last date of submission

Flora and Fauna

# 4
# Owls in the Family

## Way with Words

### Idioms Related to Birds

**A. Match each idiom related to birds to its correct meaning.**

| Idioms | Meanings |
|---|---|
| 1. night owl | a. the wanted person has escaped |
| 2. a feather in his cap | b. in a straight line |
| 3. no spring chicken | c. an achievement to be proud of |
| 4. chicken feed | d. restrict someone's freedom |
| 5. the bird has flown | e. someone who likes to stay up very late at night |
| 6. clip somebody's wings | f. a view of something from a high position |
| 7. as the crow flies | g. someone not so young |
| 8. a bird's-eye view | h. a very small amount (of money) |
| 9. chicken out | i. take care of your own interests |
| 10. feather your (own) nest | j. decide not to do something because you are afraid |

### Words with Multiple Meanings

Read the sentence.

Obviously she had no trust in me as a **foster** parent.

In the above sentence, **foster** has been used to mean a person who brings up someone else's child. However, another meaning of foster is 'to encourage or to promote the growth or development of something or someone'. The same word can have multiple meanings.

**B. Find the meanings of the following words and write a sentence using each of them.**

1. foster child ____________________
2. foster home ____________________
3. foster care ____________________

**C. Two meanings have been given for every word. Match the words with their meanings.**

| Words | Meanings |
|---|---|
| 1. cut | a. add spices to improve the taste of food |
| | b. spring, summer, autumn or winter |
| 2. ring | c. slice with a knife or scissors |
| | d. pebble or stone |
| 3. season | e. the outer part of a tree's trunk |
| | f. noise a dog makes |
| 4. rock | g. the sound a bell makes |
| | h. jewellery worn on fingers |
| 5. sink | i. a basin in the kitchen used for washing dirty dishes |
| | j. go back and forth on a chair |
| 6. bark | k. a small wound |
| | l. what a rock does in water |

## Grammar in Use

### Subject and Predicate

Every sentence has two parts – a subject and a predicate. The subject is what (or whom) the sentence is about, while the predicate tells us something about the subject.

**Examples:** **Rohit** *swims.*

**Rohit and his brother** *swim everyday.*

The highlighted words in these sentences are the subjects and the words in italics are the predicates.

**A. Circle the subject and underline the predicate in the following sentences.**

1. The boy loves the dog.
2. The hunter caught the tiger.
3. The ship was named *Beauty*.
4. The girl plays the guitar well.
5. Take this message to the office.
6. The sun was sinking behind the mountain.

## Types of Sentences

There are four types of sentences.

1. **Assertive sentences** make statements or express opinions.
   **Examples:** That house is beautiful.
   I love butter and jam on toast.
2. **Imperative sentences** are used to give commands or instructions, or to make requests.
   **Examples:** Finish your work quickly. (instruction)
   Please close the door. (request)
3. **Interrogative sentences** ask questions and end with question marks.
   **Examples:** When are you leaving?
   What is the matter?
4. **Exclamatory sentences** express strong emotions and end with exclamation marks.
   **Examples:** What a tasty meal!
   How I wish I were rich!

**A. Identify the sentences as assertive (A), imperative (Imp), interrogative (Int) or exclamatory (E).**

1. How beautiful this painting is! ______
2. Should he take a risk like this? ______
3. It is foolish to do this. ______
4. Don't take another step forward. ______
5. I hope India can produce more Olympians. ______
6. Please come with me. ______
7. That pen is mine. ______
8. How dark the clouds are! ______
9. Do you know the name of our new teacher? ______
10. We are studying for our mid-term exams. ______

**B. Respond to each situation as suggested. Write your response below each sentence.**

1. Your friend is wearing a beautiful scarf. (exclaim, admiring the scarf)
   ______
2. Your friend is feeling unwell. (ask him/her if he/she needs help)
   ______
3. Your brother is about to run across a busy road. (instruct/warn him not to)
   ______
4. Your teacher asks you what you plan to do during your holidays. (tell her)
   ______
5. Your dog is very excited and barks loudly. (order it to stop)
   ______
6. You seek permission from your mother to go on a school picnic. (ask her)
   ______

7. Your friend wants to know whether you like the cake she brought for lunch. (tell her)

8. Your parents have bought a new red car. (exclaim about its colour)

## Listening and Speaking

**Listen to this poem about an owl. Discuss in groups and answer the questions orally.**

1. Name one sound that is typically associated with owls.
2. Find a word that rhymes with **oak**.
3. What is the meaning of the line 'The less he spoke, the more he heard'? Who is being referred to as 'he' here?
4. What is the message of the poem?
5. Speak for two minutes on the adage: **Silence is Golden**.

## Pen it Down

**Write an essay on any one of the following topics.**

- an aviary
- a zoo
- an owl barn in a farm

You can use the following points in your essay:

- describe events or experiences from your own life
- think about the place and then describe it well
- use details to engage the five senses of readers: sight, hearing, touch, smell and taste
- try to draw a clear picture with your words so readers can imagine what you wish to describe
- use your imagination to add interest

# 5 Word Balloon

## Way with Words

### Word Families

**A. Complete the sentences using the correct form of the words given in brackets.**

1. One should look at people ________________ when talking to them. (direct)
2. Do not take important ________________ in a hurry. (decide)
3. Actors are ________________ people. (create)
4. Venu is always ________________ of the other politicians. (critic)
5. We ________________ our houses on special occasions, such as Christmas, Diwali, birthdays and my parents' anniversary. (decorative)
6. ________________ is the best policy. (honest)
7. Switch off the lights and the fans when they are not in use to save ________________. (electric)
8. I ________________ the film to be better. (expectations)
9. I am not ________________ to stay up late at night. (allow)
10. ________________ changes every season. (fashionable)

### Idiomatic Expressions with Time

**B. Choose the correct expressions from the box to complete the given sentences.**

| | | | |
|---|---|---|---|
| in time | pressed for time | a race against time | time on our hands |
| take your time | high time | not the time | lost track of time |
| | ahead of his/her time | behind the times | |

1. There's ____________ to save the world's remaining rainforests.
2. You have been without a job for many months now. It's ____________ you got a job!
3. He was so engrossed in his work that he ____________.
4. The team managed well and got everything finished ____________.
5. Our exams are coming up. This is ____________ to take it easy.
6. I'm a bit ____________ at the moment. Would you mind if we met next week?
7. He's definitely ____________. He's always got such out of the box ideas.

8. He's so __________. He still listens to his old radio!
9. __________ in answering the question.
10. We've got a bit of __________. Would you like to do some sightseeing?

## Grammar in Use

### Nouns: Number and Gender

**A. Rewrite each sentence using the correct form of the underlined nouns.**

1. All the child came to see the magician.
2. The woodcutter cut down a whole forest of tree.
3. Henry's father gave him two pastry.
4. When the sculptor's hammers hit the rock, there were chips and dust flying everywhere.
5. The magician performed many trick.
6. Do you know how many planet there are in our solar system?

**B. Write the masculine or feminine nouns for the animals below.**

| Animal | Masculine | Feminine |
|---|---|---|
| cat | | |
| pig | | |
| horse | | |
| tiger | | |
| lion | | |
| deer | | |
| sheep | | |
| cattle | | |

### Nouns: Countable and Uncountable

You know that nouns can be countable or uncountable.

**Examples:** an apple, two apples, three apples (countable nouns)
air, rice, water (uncountable nouns)

**C. Write C for countable and U for uncountable nouns.**

1. time ________
2. bread ________
3. water________
4. sugar ________
5. peanuts ________
6. leaves ________
7. hair ________
8. tables ________
9. eggs ________
10. butter ________
11. jam ________
12. songs ________
13. fingers ________
14. salt ________
15. bananas ________
16. trucks ________

### Transitive and Intransitive Verbs

A transitive verb requires an object to complete the meaning of a sentence. An intransitive verb does not require an object to complete the meaning of a sentence.

**Examples:** The girl wrote a poem. (object: poem)
The hot-air balloon landed safely. (no object)

**D. State whether the verbs in these sentences are transitive or intransitive.**

1. It is important to speak the truth.

________________________________________

2. The birds are flying in the sky.

________________________________________

3. The bus stopped suddenly.

________________________________________

4. Heat expands metals.

________________________________________

5. The bus driver stopped the bus.

________________________________________

6. We must not speak loudly.

________________________________________

7. *The Titanic* hit an iceberg and sank.

________________________________________

8. Metals expand on heating.

________________________________________

9. The boy fell off the pony and started crying.

________________________________________

10. The explosion shook the nearby buildings.

________________________________________

11. The boy is riding a pony.

________________________________________

12. Roses are red.

________________________________________

## Listening and Speaking

**Choose a student. He/She will talk about an object that the teacher will choose. The other students must listen carefully. The teacher can stop the student mid-sentence and ask another student to continue, using the last spoken word.**

## Pen it Down

**Think of a hot-air balloon drifting away in the sky. Think of a bird, the wind and an aeroplane. Write a short poem that brings out the element of freedom through all the four objects. Try to use the *abab* rhyme scheme. Here are some rhyming words that you can use as clues.**

1. balloon – soon – moon
2. bird – skirt – shirt – third
3. wind – grinned – winged
4. aeroplane – lane – again

Transport

# 6 Palanquin Bearers

## Way with Words

### Similes

**A. Use the ideas conveyed by the phrases and make sentences using similes. One is done for you.**

1. a swaying flower
   *The flower swayed like a sleepy child standing on its feet.*
2. a flying bird
   ______________________________
3. a foamy stream
   ______________________________
4. a teary bride
   ______________________________
5. a light laugh
   ______________________________
6. a hanging star
   ______________________________
7. a windy song
   ______________________________

### Modern Forms of Transport

**B. Use these clues to complete the crossword on the next page.**

**Across**

2. a transport system used in the mountains (5, 3)
5. a vehicle or a machine designed for travelling to outer space (10)
9. a number of carriages connected together and pulled by an engine along a railway track (5)
10. a comfortably equipped single-decker bus used for longer journeys (5)

**Down**

1. a medium-sized sailing boat equipped for cruising or racing (5)
3. a powered flying vehicle with fixed wings (9)

4. a two-wheeled vehicle that has no pedals (10)
6. an underground railway system in a city (5)
7. a four-wheeled road vehicle (3)
8. used for transporting people or goods by sea (4)

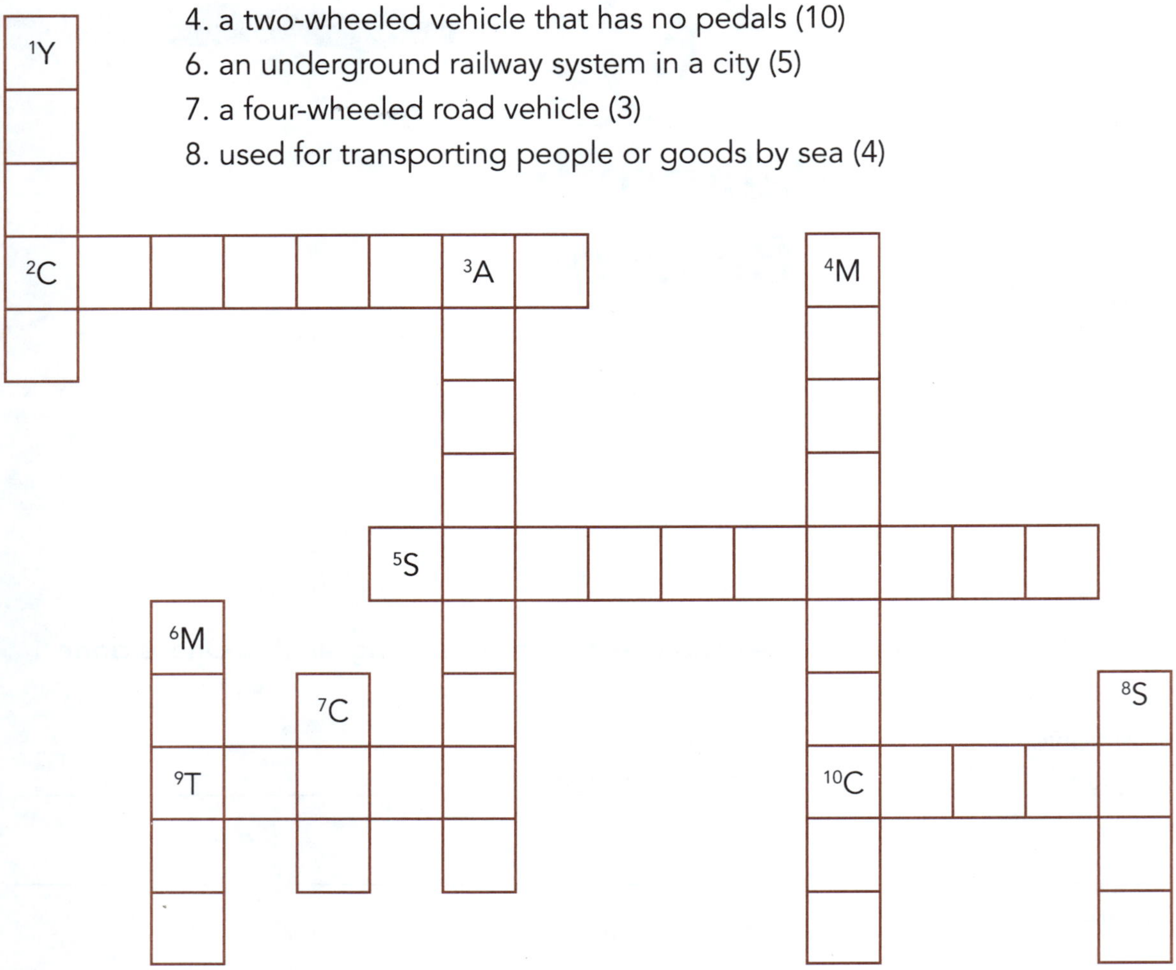


## Grammar in Use

### Infinitives and Gerunds

You know that an **infinitive** is a verb that takes the form **to** + verb. It should not be confused with the preposition **to** that is always followed by nouns and pronouns.

**Examples:** I want **to ride** on a palanquin. (infinitive)
Let us drive **to** the city. (preposition)

A **gerund** is a type of verb that takes the form verb + **-ing**. It performs the function of a noun in a sentence.

**Example:** **Driving** a car is a common mode of transport.

**A. Fill in the blanks with the infinitive or gerund form of the given verbs.**

1. ________________ (dance) is a great exercise and a fun activity.

2. Raheal wants ________________________ (be) an astronaut.

3. ________________________ (sing) is my mother's favourite pastime.

4. It is wise ________________________ (complete) one's homework every day.

5. Sheena likes ________________________ (read) comics between classes.

6. ________________________ (get) good marks is not an easy task.

7. Rama is determined ________________________ (win) the school elections.

8. It is very disappointing ________________________ (lose) to a weaker team.

### Types of Adjectives

You know that adjectives are of four main types.

**Adjectives of quantity:** tell us about the amount of a noun or pronoun.

**Example:** Please give me **some** sugar.

**Adjectives of quality:** describe the noun or pronoun.

**Example:** Rama lives in a **big** house.

**Demonstrative adjectives:** point out a noun or pronoun.

**Example:** Who is **that** boy?

**Interrogative adjectives:** ask questions about a noun or pronoun.

**Example:** **Which** car does your mother drive?

**B. Complete the sentences with the correct adjectives from the box and state their types.**

| many | much | which | these | talented | whose | those | high |
|---|---|---|---|---|---|---|---|

1. Meena is a ______________ artist with a bright future ahead of her. ______________
2. ______________ coat did you take from the coat rack? ______________
3. The cat could not reach the milk, which was on a ______________ shelf. ______________
4. Why are the trees on this side of the road greener than ______________ trees?______________
5. How ______________ milk would you like in your tea? ______________
6. Here, take ______________ strawberries. They are so juicy and sweet! ______________
7. I have ______________ *Tintin* and *Asterix* comics at home. ______________
8. ______________ gaming console would you like to buy? ______________

## Listening and Speaking

**Story Starter**

Most stories begin in a particular way. These are called story starters.
**Example:** I woke up one morning to find myself ...

**A. As a class, make a list of story starter ideas and, in turns, write them on the board.**

**B. Form groups of five and sit in a circle. The teacher will give each group a story starter from the list that was prepared. Add one sentence each to the story. After one person is done, the person sitting to his/her left adds a line from wherever the first person left off. Continue adding one sentence at a time, until the teacher gives the signal to stop. Whoever is in the middle of his/her sentence when the teacher signals, is out and must leave the circle. The story continues until only one student is left. Have a class discussion on what you learnt from this experience.**

## Pen it Down

**Imagine you are in a palanquin that is being carried by the palanquin bearers mentioned in the poem. The palanquin bearers are singing as they walk. Write an autobiographical essay describing your experience.**

You may include the following points.

- how many palanquin bearers were there
- what they were wearing
- what song they were singing
- the places you passed on your way
- how you felt about being carried in a palanquin
- a little background about your life till that point

# 7 Painting the Breeze

## Comprehension

**Read this poem and answer the questions.**

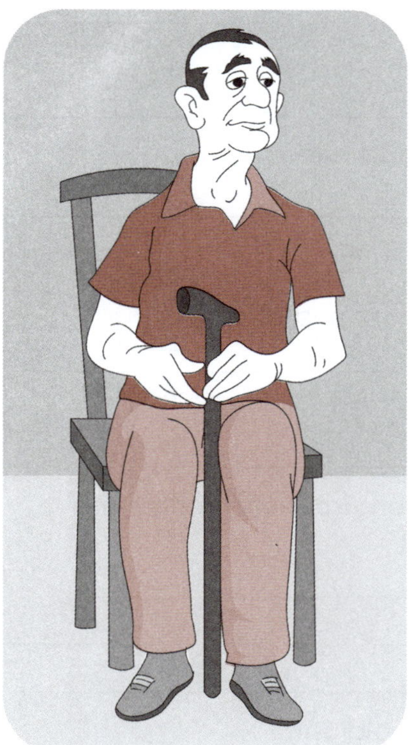

Crabbed Age and Youth
Cannot live together:
Youth is full of pleasance,
Age is full of care;
Youth like summer morn,
Age like winter weather;
Youth like summer brave,
Age like winter bare.
Youth is full of sport,
Age's breath is short;
Youth is nimble, Age is lame;
Youth is hot and bold,
Age is weak and cold;
Youth is wild and Age is tame.
Age, I do abhor thee;
Youth I do adore thee;
O, my Love, my Love is young!
Age, I do defy thee:
O, sweet shepherd, hie thee!
For methinks thou stay'st too long.

**A. Fill in the blanks with the correct options.**

1. *Abhor* and *adore* are ____________
   a. antonyms. b. synonyms. c. anagrams.

2. The poet compares age to ____________

a. winter. b. summer. c. autumn.

3. According to the poet, young people can move ____________

a. slowly. b. fast. c. lazily.

4. Youth has been compared to ____________

a. evening. b. morning. c. afternoon.

5. ____________ takes risks.

a. Old age b. Middle age c. Youth

**B. Find lines from the poem that mean the following:**

1. Youth is filled with joy.

_______________________________________________

2. Young people are carefree.

_______________________________________________

3. Old people are filled with worries.

_______________________________________________

4. The speaker expressing his wish to stay young forever.

_______________________________________________

5. Old age is compared to the time when the Earth looks bleak and barren.

_______________________________________________

**C. Answer the questions in a few lines.**

1. According to the poet, what are some differences between youth and old age?

_______________________________________________

2. Explain this line: *Youth is wild and Age is tame.*

_______________________________________________

3. The poem seems to convey that age and youth are very different from each other and cannot coexist. Do you agree with this idea? Give reasons.

_______________________________________________

_______________________________________________

_______________________________________________

4. Identify some phrases from the poem that describe youth and old age.

_______________________________________________

_______________________________________________

5. Identify pairs of rhyming words in the poem and write them here.

_______________________________________________

_______________________________________________

6. Identify a few abstract nouns appearing in the poem and write them here.

_______________________________________________

_______________________________________________

## Way with Words

### Riddles

**A. Solve these riddles by filling in the blanks with the help of the given clues.**

1. I show you the entire world. Everything is marked on me on a single sheet. I am a m ___ ___.
2. I am called the land of kangaroos. I am A ___ ___ ___ ___ ___ ___ ___ ___ ___.
3. I am the land of the midnight sun. I am N ___ ___ ___ ___ ___.
4. I am a bird that swims but cannot fly. I am a p ___ ___ ___ ___ ___ ___ ___.
5. I am the largest living bird found in the deserts of Africa. I am an o ___ ___ ___ ___ ___ ___.
6. I am a large land animal. I am also called the ship of the desert. I am a c ___ ___ ___ ___.
7. I am a story written about the life of someone by someone else.
   I am a b ___ ___ ___ ___ ___ ___ ___ ___.
8. I am a book with the synonyms of words. I am a the ___ ___ ___ r ___ s.

### Multiple Meanings of a Verb

You know that words can have multiple meanings. For example, the verb **get** can be used in a number of ways having multiple meanings.

**B. Match the columns to indicate the kind of action the verb get denotes in column A.**

| A | B |
|---|---|
| 1. It is getting dark outside. | a. scored |
| 2. I got my passport last week. | b. received |
| 3. She got a new dress from the mall. | c. arrived |
| 4. I got the highest marks in English. | d. understand |
| 5. I got home at midnight. | e. bought |
| 6. She didn't get half of the things I told her. | f. becoming |

## Grammar in Use

### Collective Nouns

You know that a collective noun refers to a group of people, animals or things.

**Examples:** an **army** of soldiers
a **flight** of butterflies

**A. Circle the correct collective noun in each sentence.**

1. An array/ambush of tigers lazed in the tall grass of the forest reserve.
2. Flocks/Colonies of ants marched through the forest carrying food.
3. Flights/Packs of wolves howled at the full moon as the woods came alive with strange and magical creatures.
4. Many classes/troops in the school were given an assignment on the protection of wildlife.
5. Flights/Clans of birds migrate to warmer environments to escape the cold during winter.
6. The caravan/herd of camels is carrying sacks of grain.
7. He has a large drove/brood of chickens.
8. The kitten was chased by a flock/murder of crows.
9. He photographed a pride/school of lions.
10. Look at the fleet/tribe of monkeys hanging from the branches.

**B. Match the columns to complete the sentences with collective nouns.**

| A | B |
|---|---|
| 1. A school | a. of thieves stole the crown jewels. |
| 2. A battery | b. of brown kittens looked for milk. |
| 3. A litter | c. of juicy grapes makes for a lovely dessert. |
| 4. The gaggle | d. of wild elephants chased the tourists. |
| 5. A bunch | e. of tests was ordered by the doctor. |
| 6. The herd | f. of geese squawked loudly. |
| 7. A band | g. of fish swam gracefully in the pond. |

## Conditional Sentences Using If and Unless

The condition in a sentence is not fulfilled unless the action in it is completed.

**Examples: If** Parvati and Laxman work hard, they will be able to support their sick father.
**Unless** the quality of clay is good, the pots will not turn out well.

**C. Complete the sentences using if or unless.**

1. ________ you stop lying, you'll get into trouble one day.
2. I won't be able to do the work ________ you help me.
3. ________ you're late, you will miss the train.
4. ________ you stop making that noise, I'll call the teacher.
5. ________ he gets caught, he will be in a fix.
6. ________ the bank pays up, we're going to have a major problem.
7. ________ we get the cheque today, we must deposit it in the bank.
8. Priti will never agree to do the role ________ you accept her suggestions.
9. I don't want to go out ________ it's raining.
10. We'll be in trouble ________ the play is not liked by the audience.

## Listening and Speaking

A. **Listen to your teacher as she reads out the steps to make sustainable earthen lamps. Now answer these questions.**

1. What is the first step in making earthen lamps?
2. Why do we need to use water with the clay?
3. Why should you not make the lamps too thin?
4. Where will you dry the lamps?
5. How will you decorate the lamps?

**If you have a chance to create something else, what would you like to make? Speak about it in class in a few lines.**

B. **Divide the class into two groups and have a debate on the topic 'Supporting products made by local artisans helps the economy and not buying mass-produced goods.' One group should speak for the motion and the other should speak against it. Based on the arguments presented, let your teacher declare if the motion is passed or not.**

## Pen it Down

**Write an essay about how children and parents need to support each other in their day-to-day lives.**

You can include the following points:

- the duties and responsibilities of parents
- the responsibilities of children in a household
- what issues lead to conflict and how they can be resolved
- ways in which children can take on more responsibilities at home so that parents do not feel overburdened
- how can parents be more mindful of the issues faced by their children

# 8 The Snail

## Way with Words

### Animal Idioms

**A. Complete the idioms in column A with the correct animal names. Then, match them with their definitions in column B.**

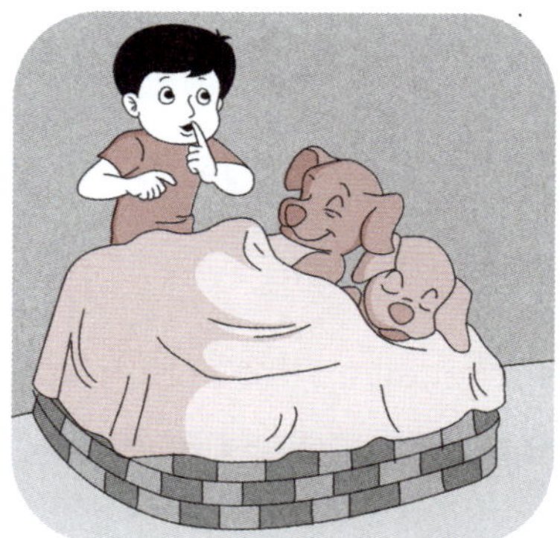

**A**

1. take the __________ by the horns
2. do the __________ work
3. flog a dead __________
4. let sleeping __________ (*plural*) lie
5. let the __________ out of the bag
6. have other __________ to fry
7. smell a __________
8. have a __________ in your bonnet

**B**

a. ignore a problem because trying to deal with it could cause an even more difficult situation
b. talk and think a lot about something
c. do the hard, boring part of a task
d. have more important or more interesting things to do
e. face a difficult or dangerous situation directly and with courage
f. sense that something is wrong about a situation
g. reveal a secret
h. waste time doing something which will not succeed

## Similes

**B. Complete the similes in the sentences using the names of the animals given in the box.**

| mouse | bee | mule | bird | ox | bat | snail | dog | lamb | eels |
|---|---|---|---|---|---|---|---|---|---|

1. Do not expect Meeta to change her mind. She is as stubborn as a ______.
2. I cannot go to school today. I am feeling as sick as a ______.
3. My brother will help you carry that heavy box up the stairs. He is as strong as an ______.
4. My grandmother cannot see anything without her glasses. She is as blind as a ______ without them.
5. My mother is always working; she is as busy as a ______.
6. Our computer at home is as slow as a ______. Father has finally agreed to buy a new one.
7. My uncle likes travelling from place to place, as free as a ______.
8. My father came to the room as quietly as a ______ and caught us playing video games.
9. My mother never shouts at my brother and me. She is as gentle as a ______.
10. The police are having a tough time catching the thieves. They are as slippery as ______.

# Grammar in Use

## Direct and Indirect Object

A **direct object** receives the action of a verb and answers the questions 'what' or 'whom'.

**Example:** The child <u>cuddles</u> her **teddy bear.**

cuddles ↓ verb; teddy bear ↓ direct object

*What does the child cuddle?* Answer: *teddy bear*

An **indirect object** receives the action of the direct object and answers the questions, 'to whom/what' or 'for whom/what'.

**Example:** The child <u>threw</u> her <u>teddy bear</u> to **her mother**.

threw ↓ verb; teddy bear ↓ direct object; her mother ↓ indirect object

*To whom did the child throw her teddy bear?* Answer: *her mother*

**Identify whether the words in bold are direct objects or indirect objects.**

1. She sent **her friend** a birthday invitation. __________
2. The maid will help **you** with your housework. __________
3. Where did you put the **milk**? __________
4. Grandmother gave **them** a bag full of oranges. __________

5. Please send **me** Bipan Chandra's book, *India's Struggle for Independence: 1857-1947* via courier. ___________
6. I need **your advice**. ___________
7. He offered her **a seat**. ___________
8. My father bought **us** a new car. ___________
9. Our neighbours gave us their **plants**. ___________
10. I wish **you** best of luck for your new venture. ___________

## Listening and Speaking

**Listen to the jokes and answer the questions.**

1. Can you repeat all the jokes in the same order?
2. Can you repeat all the jokes in a different order from the sequence in which they are given?
3. What is funny about the joke on a lettuce?
4. Which joke did you find the funniest? Why?
5. What is funny about the joke on a ladder?

## Pen it Down

**Imagine that you are a snail. Write your autobiography in the form of a poem. Make the autobiography interesting by mentioning some funny incidents that have happened to you. Ensure that you highlight the qualities and physical features of a snail, which you learnt from the poem in your coursebook.**

# 9 Tom Paints the Fence

## Way with Words

### PREFIXES AND SUFFIXES

**A. Form words with the prefixes and suffixes given below. For each word formed, write whether it is a noun, an adjective or a verb. One is done for you.**

1. *aero* + *plane* *aeroplane (noun)*
2. tele + __________ ____________________
3. __________ + hood ____________________
4. trans + __________ ____________________
5. __________ + able ____________________
6. inter + __________ ____________________
7. __________ + ful ____________________
8. __________ + ant ____________________
9. __________ + let ____________________
10. ante + __________ ____________________

**B. Add the negative prefixes un-, dis-, im-, ir- and il- to the adjectives to form new words. Use the words to complete the sentences.**

| possible | honest | legal | sociable | reasonable |
|---|---|---|---|---|
| patient | responsible | pleasant | polite | obedient |

1. My cousins are very ________________. They never say, 'please' and 'thank you'.
2. Some people are ________________ by nature. They never tell the truth.
3. My aunt is quite ________________. She doesn't like going out or talking to new people.
4. Don't be so ________________. The baked potatoes will be ready in five minutes.
5. My friend can be really ________________ sometimes. He doesn't mind upsetting people.
6. It is ________________ solving this puzzle! I can't do it.
7. I won't ask Hina to be a part of the project. She's too ________________.
8. In some countries it's ________________ to drive under the age of 17.
9. The teacher decided to talk to the ________________ student.
10. It is not possible to argue with an ________________ person.

## Grammar in Use

### Pronouns

**Personal pronouns** are used in place of names of people or things to avoid repetition. These are **I, we, me, us, you, he, she, him, her, it, they** and **them.**

**Example:** Meena had a new haircut. **She** received compliments for it.

**Possessive pronouns** are used to show ownership of something or someone. These are **mine, ours, yours, his, hers,**and **theirs.**

**Example:** I think the bag over there is **his.**

Look at these sentences.

This house is **mine.**

This is **my** house.

The word **mine** shows ownership of the noun house. It is a possessive pronoun.

The word **my** tells us more about the noun house. It is a possessive adjective.

**A. Complete the sentences using correct personal pronouns in place of the words in brackets.**

1. My grandparents live in London. (My grandparents) ____________ often come to visit us.
2. Smita, Arun, Vicky and Leela are my cousins. (Smita, Arun, Vicky and Leela) ____________ live in Kolkata.
3. I bought this pen yesterday. (The pen) ____________ writes well.
4. My sister Jane loves books. This novel is for (Jane) ____________.
5. My parents like Latin music. The CD is for (my parents) ____________.
6. My wife and I love sweets. These sweets are for (my wife and I) ____________.
7. I got off the train and found my brother waiting for (I) ____________.
8. ____________ (my parents and I) are going to China during the winter vacation.

**B. Complete the sentences with the correct pronouns.**

1. This book is ____________. (you/yours)
2. The ball is ____________. (mine/I)
3. The blue car is ____________. (our/ours)
4. The ring is ____________. (hers/her)
5. It was not my fault. It was ____________. (yours/your)
6. This house is ____________ (their/theirs).

## Listening and Speaking

**Divide the class into four groups. Each group will pick out two paragraphs from the story 'Tom Paints the Fence'. Now, the group members will take turns to read out the paragraphs. While reading, try to use the correct tones. While one group is reading, the other groups will listen carefully.**

**After they have finished reading, the group members will close their books. The other three groups will ask questions related to the story to the group that has finished reading it. Take turns in groups to read the story, and ask and answer questions based on it.**

## Pen it Down

**Imagine you are Tom. Write a descriptive account about the day you set about to paint the fence. Make it interesting and entertaining.**

You can use the following points:

- why you had to paint the fence
- your thoughts at the beginning
- how you tried to get out of it
- what idea you finally had
- how you tricked your friends
- your aunt's reaction

# Test Paper

## Comprehension

**Read the poem 'We are Seven' by William Wordsworth and answer the questions.**

I met a little cottage Girl:
She was eight years old, she said;
Her hair was thick with many a curl
That clustered round her head.

She had a rustic, woodland air,
And she was wildly clad:
Her eyes were fair, and very fair;
Her beauty made me glad.

'Sisters and brothers, little Maid,
How many may you be?'
'How many? Seven in all,' she said
And wondering looked at me.

'And where are they? I pray you tell.'
She answered, 'Seven are we;
And two of us at Conway dwell,
And two are gone to sea.

'Two of us in the church-yard lie,
My sister and my brother;
And, in the church-yard cottage, I
Dwell near them with my mother.'

**A. State whether the statements are true (T) or false (F).**

1. The poet met a little girl who lived in the city. __________
2. The girl was eight years old. __________
3. The little girl's siblings had all gone to the sea. __________
4. Two of the girl's siblings lived at Conway. __________
5. Three of the girl's siblings had died. __________

**B. Which lines in the poem express the following ideas?**

1. The little girl was dressed untidily.

________________________________________

2. The girl gave the poet a surprised look.

3. The poet requested the girl to tell him about her siblings.

4. The girl lived in a cottage with her mother.

**C. Answer these questions in a few lines.**

1. Describe the girl the poet had met. What about her made the poet happy?

2. How many siblings did the girl have? Where did they live?

3. Where did the girl live?

4. Pick out the rhyming words from the poem. Write three more rhyming words for each set of words.

5. Which word has been repeated in the poem? What effect does it create?

## Way with Words

**A. Make sentences with these similes.**

1. as bright as a button
2. like cats and dogs
3. as thin as a rail
4. like a glove
5. as white as a ghost

**B. Write the meanings of these idioms.**

1. as the crow flies
2. hold one's horses
3. a feather in his cap

4. get the lion's share ______________________________
5. clam up ______________________________

**C. Rewrite these sentences using the correct synonyms of the underlined words. Choose from the words given in the brackets.**

1. You have <u>recently</u> painted the fence. (lately/often/freshly)
______________________________
2. Dogs have a <u>keen</u> sense of smell. (blunt/sharp/eager)
______________________________
3. I really <u>admire</u> her courage. (like/hate/respect)
______________________________
4. His parents were very <u>anxious</u> about his wellbeing. (worried/confused/uncertain)
______________________________
5. She visits her grandparents <u>frequently</u>. (occasionally/often/never)
______________________________

**D. Choose the option that is opposite in meaning to these words.**

1. arrogant
   a. shy ☐ b. confident ☐ c. modest ☐
2. constant
   a. variable ☐ b. habitual ☐ c. active ☐
3. concise
   a. brief ☐ b. lengthy ☐ c. lean ☐
4. loathe
   a. cherish ☐ b. hate ☐ c. reject ☐
5. primitive
   a. elementary ☐ b. old ☐ c. modern ☐

**E. Add suffixes to the words within brackets to form meaningful sentences.**

1. Be (care) while crossing the road.
______________________________
2. The (art) made a beautiful portrait.
______________________________
3. I finally received (compensate) for my hard work.
______________________________
4. Scientists are (doubt) about the origin of the rock.
______________________________
5. Our team has won the (champion) three years in a row.
______________________________

## Grammar in Use

**A. Identify the gender of these nouns and write them in the space provided.**

1. uncle ______________
2. neighbour ______________
3. tree ______________
4. lady ______________
5. heiress ______________
6. doctor ______________
7. gold ______________
8. author ______________
9. bird ______________
10. rice ______________

**B. Circle the subjects and underline the predicates in these sentences.**

1. The beautiful bird has made a small nest in the tree.
2. P. V. Sindhu won the bronze medal at the Tokyo 2020 Olympic games.
3. The boy and his friends went to the restaurant nearby.
4. Those paintings have not been made by our art teacher.
5. Swimming is an activity that Ajay enjoys.

**C. Rewrite these sentences correctly using the plural forms of the underlined nouns. You may make other necessary changes.**

1. The pack of wolf attacked the hunter.

   ______________________________________________

2. The lady was wearing expensive dresses.

   ______________________________________________

3. The dentist wanted to extract two of his tooth.

   ______________________________________________

4. Both his foot were injured in the accident.

   ______________________________________________

5. You can get the latest news on television.

   ______________________________________________

**D. Convert these sentences as instructed in the brackets.**

1. I am going to visit him tomorrow. (interrogative)

   ______________________________________________

2. He is a dishonest person. (negative)

   ______________________________________________

3. Birds of different feathers do not flock together. (positive)

   ______________________________________________

4. We have won the trophy. (exclamatory)

   ______________________________________________

5. My father is a doctor. (interrogative)

   ______________________________________________

**E. Complete these sentences using collective nouns.**

1. I presented her with a __________ of flowers on her birthday.
2. He gathered a __________ of juicy grapes from the vine.
3. A __________ of sheep was grazing in the field.
4. A long __________ of steps led to the top of the tower.
5. The __________ of soldiers fought bravely with the enemy.

**F. Circle the transitive verbs in the sentences and underline their objects. Say whether they are direct or indirect objects.**

1. Seema sold her old furniture to the scrap dealer.
2. I like to eat oranges.
3. The cricket ball broke the front glass of our car.
4. My grandfather sometimes reads the newspaper to me.
5. I am watching a cartoon film.

**G. Complete these sentences using possessive pronouns.**

1. Do you see that brown dog? I adopted it from the shelter. It is __________.
2. I bought my sister some toys. These dolls are __________.
3. Pick any of the pens. The choice is __________.
4. My uncle and aunt have come for a visit. The car parked outside is __________.
5. We live in this building. The flat on the fifth floor is __________.

## Listening and Speaking

**Imagine that you have found an invisibility cloak in the attic of your house. Tell the class about how you are going to use the cloak. Try to make your description imaginative and funny.**

## Pen it Down

**A. You have been on a holiday with your friends to a hill station. Write a diary entry on any one of the days you spent there.**

You can include the following points:

- how the day started
- the places you planned to visit
- the weather on that day
- the interesting things you saw on your way
- any exciting occurrence

**B. Write a short story beginning with:**

*Today, I again dreamt of that bear ...*

**Give your story a suitable title.**

C. Write an article for a newspaper on the rising levels of pollution in your city, the causes and how they adversely affect your daily life. Give any suggestions that you have on how to control the menace.

# 10

# I am Malala

## Comprehension

**Read this passage and answer the questions.**

The Rio Grande is not the longest river in America, but it ranks among the most important rivers in the country. The reason for that is its location. The river has been serving as the official border between Texas, USA, and Mexico since 1846. The literal meaning of Rio Grande is 'Big River'. However, the river is known in Mexico as Rio Bravo. This translates into the 'furious river'. The name is quite suitable too. The river seems to be in a terrible rage, because of its curving route and sharp twists and turns.

The Rio Grande is the fourth or the fifth longest river in America. This varies according to the varying length of the river. As the river twists so much, it frequently changes its course and its length. Officially, it is 1896 miles in length. The river starts in Colorado and has its mouth in the Gulf of Mexico. 'Downwards' is the best word to describe the movement of the river. It flows from north to south as well as from high mountains to lower lands before plunging into the gulf.

The Rio Grande is also unique as unlike most other big rivers, this river cannot be navigated by ocean-going vehicles. The river is mostly used as a source of drinking water. However, it is slowly drying up. Parts of it are already dry. This has been caused by the people using more water than the river can get back. Experts are engaged in trying to solve this problem.

Perhaps the greatest significance of the river is that it is a symbol of cooperation between the people of Mexico and Texas. The water of the river is used by the people on either side of the border. It acts as a border but also as a common space. Today, the Rio Grande stands as the symbol of peace and friendship between the two nations and their people.

**A. State whether the statements are true (T) or false (F).**

1. The Rio Grande is the official border between North America and Mexico. _______
2. The Rio Grande is the longest river of North America. _______
3. The river starts in Colorado and ends in the Gulf of Mexico. _______
4. Ocean-going vehicles can move very fast in this river. _______
5. Parts of the river have become dry. _______

**B. Choose the correct options.**

1. According to the passage, why is the Rio Grande so important?
   a. It is a source of drinking water for most of America. ☐
   b. It is the border between Texas and Mexico. ☐
   c. It is the longest river system in America. ☐
   d. It is known by two different names. ☐
2. It is difficult to measure the exact length of the Rio Grande because
   a. it seems to be very angry. ☐
   b. it is a very long river. ☐
   c. it shifts its course frequently. ☐
   d. most of the river is dry. ☐
3. Why is 'downwards' the best way of describing the river?
   a. It extends from east to west. ☐
   b. It provides water to Mexico, which is to the south of America. ☐
   c. Ships cannot navigate it easily. ☐
   d. It starts high in the mountains and loses height on its course. ☐
4. The river seems to be furious because
   a. it has many twists and turns. ☐
   b. it is angrier than other rivers. ☐
   c. its name means 'furious'. ☐
   d. it makes a lot of noise. ☐
5. According to the passage, the Rio Grande has endpoints in
   a. Texas and the Gulf of Mexico. ☐
   b. New Mexico and Colorado. ☐
   c. Texas and Mexico. ☐
   d. Colorado and the Gulf of Mexico. ☐

**C. Answer the questions in a few lines.**

1. The author says that the Rio Grande is 'a symbol of cooperation' between Mexico and Texas. However, it also divides the two countries. Do you think the river is more unifying or divisive? How do you think the river symbolises cooperation?

______________________________________________

______________________________________________

______________________________________________

______________________________________________

2. Why have parts of the river dried up?

______________________________________________

______________________________________________

3. Name the states and countries mentioned in the passage.

______________________________________________

______________________________________________

4. What is the difference between the Rio Grande and other big rivers in America? What is it mostly used for?

______________________________________________

______________________________________________

## Way with Words

### Homonyms and Homophones

**Homonyms** are words that are pronounced and spelt the same but have different meanings.
**Homophones** are words that are pronounced the same but have different spellings and meanings.

**Examples:** land (homonym: a. an area of ground; b. arrive somewhere after a journey)
too - two (homophones)

**A. Read each pair of sentences and write the meanings of the highlighted words.**

1. a. My father works in a **bank**. ______________
   b. There is a temple near the **bank** of the river. ______________
2. a. I am up for a **game** of tennis. ______________
   b. The hunting of **game** birds in national parks is strictly prohibited. ______________
3. a. The meeting will **break** for informal discussions at 4 p.m. ______________
   b. It is very difficult to **break** toughened glass. ______________
4. a. She gave me a lovely **present** on my birthday. ______________
   b. At **present**, this university does not offer law courses. ______________
5. a. Please **close** the door. ______________
   b. The boy sat **close** to his uncle. ______________

**B. Complete these sentences using the correct homophones.**

1. All my friends are very ________ to me. (deer/dear)
2. Remember to be ________ when you play. (fair/fare)
3. We got ________ for the pizzas we didn't order. (build/billed)

4. The driver applied the ________ immediately and brought the speeding car to a halt. (breaks/brakes)
5. ________ you be going to the exhibition tomorrow? (Wood/Would)

## Grammar in Use

### Prepositions

A **preposition** is placed before a noun or a pronoun to indicate its relation to other words in the sentence.

**Examples:** The book is **on** the table.
We can meet **at** the bus stop.

**A. Complete the sentences using appropriate prepositions.**

1. They crossed the border ________ the cover ________ darkness.
2. ________ reference ________ your letter, this is to inform you that you have been granted leave.
3. I can't accept your invitation owing ________ a prior engagement.
4. I was ________ the phone when the bell rang.
5. She did not want to borrow ________ her grandmother.
6. The miners dug out coal ________ beneath the Earth.
7. I'll see you ________ the conference.
8. We sat down ________ the grass and had our lunch.
9. My parents got married ________ the 1990s.
10. There's a good restaurant ________ the end of the street.
11. We usually have lots of sweets ________ Diwali.
12. I would like to travel ________ Australia next summer.

### Inappropriate Shift in Tenses

The verbs used in a sentence should be in the same tense. Only if there is a change in time, should the tense shift.

**Example:** I liked concerts but I'm not able to attend any. (incorrect)
I like concerts but I'm not able to attend any. (correct)

**B. Rewrite the sentences correctly.**

1. Mohan took a paper and a pen and writes a letter to his father.
________________________________
2. A bird came and is sitting on my window pane.
________________________________
3. After my mother cooked dinner, my father serves it to the guests.
________________________________

4. I buy my tickets and then waited for the train to arrive at the station.

5. When the player hit a six, the fans go wild.

6. Priya came late for work because she is not feeling well.

## Listening and Speaking

**Listen to an extract from the book, *The Story of My Life* by Helen Keller and answer the questions.**

1. Why didn't the girl rejoice with her family after her fever was gone?

2. What signs did the girl make to communicate with others?

3. How did the girl realise that she was different from others?

4. Why was the girl angry when she stood between two persons?

## Pen it Down

Together with Malala, Kailash Satyarthi from India had received the Nobel Peace Prize for his struggle to eradicate child labour from India.

**Write an essay on the evils of child labour and how it can be abolished. You may include the following points in your essay:**

- Do you think it is right to make children work for financial gains?
- Should children work or study and play at a young age?
- Are parents right in making their children work to support the family financially?
- Should people be employing children in offices, factories and homes to save money?
- What steps can citizens and the government take to eradicate this evil from society?

Music and Creativity

# 11 The Nightingale

## Way with Words

### Antonyms

**A. Match the words in column A with their antonyms in column B.**

| A | B |
|---|---|
| 1. delicate | a. unwilling |
| 2. lofty | b. ignorant |
| 3. elegant | c. ugly |
| 4. learned | d. energised |
| 5. beautiful | e. complicated |
| 6. tired | f. tough |
| 7. simple | g. inelegant |
| 8. willing | h. low |

### Bird Sounds

**B. Match the names of the birds to the sounds they make.**

| Bird | Sound |
|---|---|
| 1. pigeon | a. screech |
| 2. crow | b. coo |
| 3. parrot | c. caw |
| 4. hummingbird | d. chirp |
| 5. lark | e. chatter |
| 6. magpie | f. sing |
| 7. sparrow | g. hum |

## Grammar in Use

### Simple and Continuous Tenses

The **simple present tense** is used to describe habits and universal truths.
**Example:** My mother **cooks** pasta.
The **simple past tense** describes an action that started and ended in the past.
**Example:** I **had** a maths test yesterday.
The **simple future tense** is used to describe an action that will take place in the future.
**Example:** Ranjeev **will run** a half marathon tomorrow.
The **present continuous tense** is used to describe an action that is going on at present.
**Example:** Veena **is painting** a portrait now.
The **past continuous tense** is used to describe an action that was going on for a while in the past.
**Example:** I **was running** in the park last evening when you called.
The **future continuous tense** is used to describe an action that will go on for a while in the future.
**Example:** Fatima **will be staying** in the youth hostel next month.

**A. Tick (✓) the correct form of the verbs given in brackets.**

1. My father will (leave/left) for the US tomorrow.
2. The robots (take/took) control of Earth.
3. We shall find the person who (will steal/stole) the money.
4. The cat (hide/hides) under the table when visitors come.
5. I (kept/keep) my bag in the classroom before I (go/went) out to play yesterday.
6. Who (will open/opened) the batting in the match tomorrow?
7. The team (loses/lost) five test matches in a row.
8. Do you (agreed/agree) that honesty is the best policy?
9. At first the root (grow/grows) and then it (supports/support) the plant.
10. The party (went/goes) on till well past midnight.

**B. Complete the sentences using the correct form of the verbs given in brackets.**

1. Hark! Rupali ______________ (sing) again. She often ______________ (sing) this song.
2. My father ______________ (have) a lot of work to do every weekend.
3. The girls ______________ (not talk) now. All of them ______________ (watch) a film.
4. The children ______________ (play) the piano and ______________ (sing) a song.
5. Rohit ______________ (throw) a party today because it ______________ (be) his birthday.
6. The class ______________ (start) at 9 o'clock every morning.
7. Pooja ______________ (like) to read books during her free time.
8. The boys ______________ (swim) in the pool now, but they usually ______________ (swim) in the sea.

**C. Use the appropriate continuous tense form of the verbs in brackets to complete the sentences.**

1. My mother ______________ (clean) the store room now.
2. It ______________ (rain) heavily last evening.
3. Who ______________ he ______________ (talk) to a while ago?
4. They ______________ (watch) a movie when their friends came over.
5. We ______________ (stay) at home this weekend.
6. Alok ______________ (travel) in the metro when you called.
7. The students ______________ (sit) in the school auditorium after having lunch.
8. Why ______________ you ______________ (watch) television when you have a test tomorrow?

## Listening and Speaking

**Work in pairs. One student will have a list of proverbs written on a paper while the partner will have the meanings of these proverbs on another sheet of paper. The student with the list of proverbs will ask the meanings of the proverbs at random and the partner will then have to tell the meaning. Change roles after five proverbs.**

### Proverbs

1. No man is an island.
2. When in Rome, do as the Romans do.
3. Fortune favours the bold.
4. People living in glass houses should not throw stones at others.
5. When the going gets tough, the tough get going.
6. The pen is mightier than the sword.
7. Hope for the best but prepare for the worst.
8. Better late than never.
9. Birds of a feather flock together.
10. A picture is worth a thousand words.

### Meanings of the proverbs

1. No one can live completely in isolation. Everyone needs someone's help.
2. Act the way in which people around you are acting.
3. People who go out bravely to achieve their goals are successful.
4. Don't criticise other people if you are not perfect yourself.
5. Strong people do not give up when they come across challenges. They just work harder.
6. Trying to convince people with ideas and words is more effective than trying to force them to do what you want.
7. Things may not go your way, so be prepared.

8. It's best to do something on time. But if you can't do it on time, finish it nevertheless.
9. People like to spend time with others who are similar to them.
10. Pictures convey emotions and messages better than written or spoken explanations.

## Pen it Down

In the story 'The Nightingale', the king kept the nightingale in a cage to listen to her song. The nightingale lost her freedom but the king was entertained. Do you think the king did the right thing by keeping the nightingale in captivity for his own entertainment?

**Write an argumentative essay on the topic: Should animals and birds be kept in captivity or should they be left to live in their natural habitat? Give arguments for and against the topic and then give your opinion on it.**

# 12

Humour

# The Tale of Custard the Dragon

## Way with Words

### Metaphors

**A. Explain the metaphors in these sentences. One is done for you.**

1. The beautiful lake was a mirror.
   *The beautiful lake was clear like a mirror and was reflecting things around it like a mirror does.*
2. Sunita's life as an astronaut is a dream come true!
   ______________________________
3. Rahul is the black sheep of his family.
   ______________________________
4. There was a sea of people at the mall.
   ______________________________
5. The maths test was a murder.
   ______________________________
6. All men and women are actors on the stage of life.
   ______________________________
7. Anne is a busy bee, spending all her time in office.
   ______________________________
8. A good book is a key that unlocks your mind.
   ______________________________

### Onomatopoeia

**B. Match the objects and animals to the sounds they make.**

| Column A | Column B |
|---|---|
| 1. the sound of a sneeze | a. pitter-patter |
| 2. the sound of potatoes being fried | b. buzz |
| 3. the sound of rain | c. whoosh |
| 4. the sound of bees | d. crash |
| 5. the sound of paper | e. achoo |
| 6. the sound of a ceramic cup falling to the ground | f. crackle |
| 7. the sound of a plane taking off | g. sizzle |

### Words With Similar Meaning

**C. Identify the odd word in each set of words. Give a reason for your choice.**

| | | | | |
|---|---|---|---|---|
| 1. window | curtain | ceiling | door | gate |
| 2. cutlass | knife | sword | cleaver | bottle opener |
| 3. wagon | cart | wheelbarrow | lorry | trolley |
| 4. torch | battery | lantern | bulb | lamp |

## Grammar in Use

### Phrases and Clauses

A **phrase** is a group of words without a subject or a verb and does not make complete sense on its own.

**Examples:** as fast as possible
with black shoes

A **clause** is a group of words with a subject and a verb. It can be a sentence in itself or a part of a sentence.

**Examples:** Rita is thirsty.
I went to bed late last night, so I woke up late today.

There are two types of clauses.

A **main clause** can stand on its own as a sentence.

A **subordinate clause** has a subject and a verb, but does not convey complete meaning. It needs a main clause to make complete sense.

**Examples:** **He has a stomach ache** because he ate too much popcorn.
**She slept like a log** as she was very tired.

The clauses in bold are the main clauses and the ones that have been underlined are subordinate clauses.

**A. Underline the phrases in these sentences.**

1. The packets in the car are Diwali gifts.
2. People go for skiing in winter.
3. The girl drove the car around the block.
4. The boys sat in the back seat.
5. Adjectives and verbs are different parts of speech.
6. These street dogs bark a lot.
7. The kitten sat between my feet.
8. The teacher walked out of the class.
9. I want to have an ice cream.
10. All living things need to keep cool in summer.

**B. Identify whether these groups of words are main clauses or subordinate clauses.**

1. because she was so sure of herself ______________
2. Sonu must have fallen asleep. ______________
3. Ram made a mistake. ______________
4. although Shyam was not seriously injured ______________
5. if she had not worn her new blue dress ______________
6. Riya lay there for a while to recover. ______________
7. Rohit fell off his bicycle. ______________
8. since Anushree came early ______________
9. whenever we go for summer vacations ______________
10. The man was driving without his licence. ______________

## Listening and Speaking

**You read about a dragon whom everyone considered a coward but who turned out to be brave. Narrate to your partner a similar instance when you were afraid of something but ended up acting bravely.**

You can include the following points:

- what made you feel afraid and when
- the reaction of the people around you
- how you overcame your fear
- if anyone came to your aid and how they helped or motivated you

## Pen it Down

**Look at the picture and write a narrative essay based on what it suggests to you.**

You can include the following points:

- who are the people and what are they doing
- what might have happened before the current situation
- what might happen next

You may use other points of your own too.

# 13 Bruno Goes Exploring

## Comprehension

**Read the poem and answer the questions.**

'Little by little,' an acorn said,
As it slowly sank in its mossy bed,
'I am improving every day,
Hidden deep in the earth away.'

Little by little, each day it grew;
Little by little, it sipped the dew;
Downward it sent out a thread-like root;
Up in the air sprung a tiny shoot.

Day after day, and year after year,
Little by little the leaves appear;
And the slender branches spread far and wide,
Till the mighty oak is the forest's pride.

Far down in the depths of the dark blue sea,
An insect train work ceaselessly.
Grain by grain, they are building well,
Each one alone in its little cell.

Moment by moment, and day by day,
Never stopping to rest or to play,
Rocks upon rocks, they are rearing high,
Till the top looks out on the sunny sky.

'Little by little,' said a thoughtful boy,
'Moment by moment, I'll well employ,
Learning a little every day,
And not spending all my time in play.
And still this rule in my mind shall dwell,
Whatever I do, I will do it well.'

'Little by little, I'll learn to know
The treasured wisdom of long ago;
And one of these days, perhaps, we'll see
That the world will be the better for me;'
And do you not think that this simple plan
Made him a wise and useful man?

**A. Complete these sentences.**

1. The acorn lay in ______________.
2. The acorn sent down a ______________.
3. The acorn was ______________ every day.
4. The acorn grows into an ______________ tree.
5. The boy wants to ______________ a little every day.
6. The boy wants to do everything ______________.

**B. Answer these questions in a few lines.**

1. Explain the following lines:

   *Moment by moment, and day by day,*
   *Never stopping to rest or to play,*
   *Rocks upon rocks, they are rearing high,*
   *Till the top looks out on the sunny sky.*

   ______________________________________________
   ______________________________________________
   ______________________________________________
   ______________________________________________
   ______________________________________________
   ______________________________________________

2. Identify the lines that suggest that our actions can make the world a better place.

   ______________________________________________
   ______________________________________________
   ______________________________________________
   ______________________________________________

3. Find pairs of rhyming words in the poem. Add one word of your own to each pair.

   ______________________________________________
   ______________________________________________
   ______________________________________________
   ______________________________________________

4. Why is the oak tree considered the 'forest's pride'?

   ______________________________________________
   ______________________________________________
   ______________________________________________
   ______________________________________________

5. Why does the poet use the words 'little by little' repeatedly in the poem?

   ______________________________________________
   ______________________________________________
   ______________________________________________

## Way with Words

### Words Often Confused

**A. Circle the correct words and complete the sentences.**

1. Sami seems to be more intelligent (then/than) her sister.
2. Ria (accepted/excepted) the invitation to my birthday party.
3. Mother usually buys (to/too/two) loaves of bread at a time.
4. The children (were/we're/where) all playing cricket in the morning.
5. (It's/Its) been three days since the fair started.
6. I will try to not let her letters (affect/effect) me.
7. This (bear/bare) is almost fully covered with fur, except for some (bear/bare) patches.
8. It is understood (then/than) that there will be no exam on Monday.
9. You take (to/too/two) many chances when you are batting.
10. Everyone (accept/except) Dr Sudha agreed to perform the operation.
11. Our experiences as a child (affect/effect) our behaviour as an adult.
12. This car is really (fast/first)!

### Collocations

You know that collocations are groups of words which are used together.
**Example:** The dog has **made a mess** of the living room.

**B. Match the words to form collocations.**

| A | B |
|---|---|
| 1. take | a. in touch |
| 2. have | b. attention |
| 3. come | c. a seat |
| 4. pay | d. to a decision |
| 5. keep | e. a bath |

## Grammar in Use

### Abstract Nouns

You have learnt that **abstract nouns** refer to things which we cannot see or touch, but can only feel. They denote ideas, qualities, feelings or states of being.
**Examples:** hope, beauty

**A. Fill in the blanks with the correct abstract nouns.**

| faith | freedom | height | honesty |
|---|---|---|---|
| success | victory | courage | |

1. There is no shortcut to ____________.
2. One should never lose ____________ in any situation.
3. After a long and hard battle, Arthur finally led his soldiers to ____________.
4. ____________ is the best policy.
5. The prisoners were ecstatic to be granted ______________ by the prince.
6. What the basketball player lacks in agility, he makes up for in ____________.
7. This award is for people who have displayed ______________ in risking their own lives to save others.

### Compound Nouns

You know that a **compound noun** is formed by combining two nouns to make a completely new word. The meaning of the new word is usually different from either of its parts.
**Example:** water + proof = **waterproof**

**B. Fill in the blanks with the given compound nouns.**

| sunlight | buttercups | fireworks | bumblebee | chairperson | railway |
|---|---|---|---|---|---|

1. A _____________ stung me on the cheek while I was working in the garden.
2. The opening ceremony of the Tokyo Olympic games included a display of _____________.
3. The artist likes to paint when all the objects in the room look sharper and brighter in the _____________.
4. The ________________ will head the urban development committee and decide next year's plan for the locality.
5. The ________________ tracks led to an abandoned tunnel.
6. My mother loves _____________ more than any other flower.

### Perfect and Perfect Continuous Tenses

Look at this table to learn about the different forms of perfect and perfect continuous tenses.

| Tense | Perfect | Perfect continuous |
|---|---|---|
| **Present** | It is used to describe an action completed in the recent past, but whose effects still remain in the present.<br>**Example:** The children **have done** their homework. | It is used to describe an action that started in the past but is still going on in the present time.<br>Words like *since* (to indicate a point of time) and *for* (to indicate a period of time) are used with this tense.<br>**Example:** Bruno **has been dreaming** about Berlin since they moved here. |

| Tense | Perfect | Perfect continuous |
|---|---|---|
| **Past** | It is used to talk about a past action that was completed before another action started.<br>**Example:** He **had checked** the house before going on his exploration. | It is used to talk about an action that took place in the past and continued up to a specific time in the past.<br>**Example:** Bruno **had been going** on explorations for the past few weeks. |
| **Future** | It is used to talk about a future activity that will be finished by or before a specific time in the future.<br>**Example:** By next Sunday, Bruno **will have spent** four months here. | It is used to talk about an ongoing activity which has not yet been completed but will be at a particular time in the future.<br>**Example:** By this time next year, Bruno **will have been attending** Herr Liszt's lessons for two years. |

**C. Fill in the blanks with the perfect or perfect continuous tense of the given verbs.**

1. She is tired because she ______________ (study) very hard for the past two weeks.
2. I ______________ (write) mails all day.
3. Angelina is getting thinner because she ______________ (eat) too little.
4. I ______________ (peel) potatoes all morning.
5. Anju ______________ (attend) a stitching course since July.
6. For how long ______________ she ______________ (learn) Spanish?
7. Where are my books? I ______________ (look) for them everywhere.
8. It has been two days since the robber ______________ (escape) from the prison.
9. How long ______________ you ______________ (use) a laptop?
10. Preeti ______________ (teach) Ajay for three years.
11. She ______________ (earn) a lot of money for the last three years.
12. It ______________ (rain) since yesterday.

**D. Complete the sentences using will have + past participle form of the verbs in the brackets.**

1. Life ____________________ (become) more digital by the next century.
2. Machines ____________________ (take over) many of the jobs that people do today.
3. The Earth's supplies of natural resources ____________________ (run out) in a few decades from now.
4. Scientists ____________________ (discover) other sources of energy to meet the needs of the global population.
5. We ____________________ (find) a way to feed all the children in the world.

## Listening and Speaking

**Form pairs and take turns to introduce your partner to the other pairs. The introduction should be done in a formal manner. While introducing, remember to follow this format.**

- I would like you to meet ____________.
- He/She is fond of ____________ (reading, playing tennis/cricket/badminton or writing).
- His/Her favourite subject is ____________.

**Listen carefully to the introductions.**

## Pen it Down

Look at the person sitting next to you in class. How well do you know him/her?

**Write a short paragraph on your partner describing him/her, his/her likes and dislikes, hobbies, strengths and weaknesses.**

______________________________________________________________________

______________________________________________________________________

______________________________________________________________________

______________________________________________________________________

______________________________________________________________________

______________________________________________________________________

______________________________________________________________________

______________________________________________________________________

______________________________________________________________________

______________________________________________________________________

______________________________________________________________________

______________________________________________________________________

______________________________________________________________________

______________________________________________________________________

______________________________________________________________________

______________________________________________________________________

______________________________________________________________________

______________________________________________________________________

______________________________________________________________________

______________________________________________________________________

______________________________________________________________________

______________________________________________________________________

______________________________________________________________________

Science and Technology

# 14

# Building a Windmill

## Way with Words

### Contextual Usage

**A. Use these words and phrases from the graphic story in sentences of your own.**

1. power source ____________________
2. carry out experiments ____________________
3. swept the country ____________________
4. play a significant role ____________________
5. black fumes ____________________

### Words related to Professions

**B. Match the professions with their correct descriptions.**

| A | B |
|---|---|
| 1. This person paints buildings and houses. | a. translator |
| 2. This person writes and edits news articles. | b. salesperson |
| 3. This person plays musical instruments. | c. supervisor |
| 4. This person manages a restaurant or hotel. | d. cashier |
| 5. This person collects news for newspapers, radio or television. | e. manager |
| 6. This person fixes cars, buses and bikes. | f. journalist |
| 7. This person's job is to supervise people. | g. repairperson |
| 8. This person repairs things at home. | h. reporter |
| 9. This person translates from one language to another. | i. painter |
| 10. This person sells cars, clothes, shoes, etc. | j. waitress |
| 11. This person looks after patients. | k. musician |
| 12. This person uses a cash register at work. | l. nurse |
| 13. This person serves food at a restaurant. | m. veterinarian |
| 14. This person is a doctor for animals. | n. mechanic |

## Grammar in Use

### Active and Passive Voice

A sentence is said to be in the **active voice** if the subject is the doer of the action.

A sentence is said to be in the **passive voice** if the subject receives the action being performed.

**Examples:** Ram kicked the football. (active)
The football was kicked by Ram. (passive)

**A. Rewrite the sentences in passive voice.**

**Example:** A postman delivered this letter. (active)
This letter was delivered by a postman. (passive)

1. The contractor used red bricks to build the house.

2. You must not tell a lie.

3. They were swimming in the pool at 6 o'clock.

4. Deepa's teacher will inform her parents about the award.

5. M. F. Hussain painted this picture.

6. Has anyone switched on the air conditioner?

7. The nurse gave the patient an injection.

8. Priya's mother is baking a cake for her.

9. Our team has won the inter-school football competition.

10. We caught the thief and took him to the police station.

**B. Rewrite the sentences in active voice.**

1. This poster was made by my brother and his friend.

2. The drowning man was saved by the brave lifeguard.

3. The detective was puzzled by the difficult case.

4. This year's tennis championship was won by Roger Federer.

5. *Kidnapped* is a book written by R. L. Stevenson.

6. The deer was caught by the lion after a long chase.

7. The vaccine for rabies was invented by Louis Pasteur.

8. This book has been written by my favourite author.

9. The smuggler was arrested by the police.

10. Get the report card signed by your parents.

**C. Unjumble the words to make meaningful sentences in passive voice. You may have to change the form of some words to get the correct tense.**

**Example:** the telephone/invent/A. G. Bell
The telephone was invented by A. G. Bell.

1. in the future/big cities/block/traffic

2. each year/thousands of phones/produce/Chinese companies

3. penicillin/discover/A. Fleming/in 1928

4. a lot/US students/ pay/for university education

5. since World War I/fighter planes/use/armies all over the world

6. regarded as one/ Harry Houdini is/of all time/of the greatest magicians

7. was given/the baby panda/a kind farmer/shelter by

### Coordinating Conjunctions

You know that **coordinating conjunctions** join two or more words, phrases or clauses of equal importance in a sentence. They are **and**, **but**, **or**, **so**, **for**, **yet** and **nor**.

**Examples:** Anand **and** Lekha went on a picnic with their cousins.
Ravi might be poor, **but** he is trustworthy.

**D. Complete the sentences using the correct coordinating conjunctions from the brackets.**

1. My father has a personal assistant ________ a typist as well. (but/or/and)
2. Huma has no patience with people who are habitually late, ________ does she allow delays in work. (but/nor/or)
3. My mother wanted to go by road to Manali, ________ my father insisted that they fly. (and/or/but)
4. I'm not afraid of dogs ________ lizards. (so/yet/or)
5. I have to wake up early ________ my exams begin tomorrow. (and/nor/for)

**E. Join the sentences using coordinating conjunctions.**

1. Raina like to paint. She likes to dance.
   ______________________________________________
2. Fana wanted to throw a party. She was too excited.
   ______________________________________________
3. I had prepared well for my exams. I did poorly.
   ______________________________________________
4. Naina won't attend the seminar. She is sick.
   ______________________________________________
5. The students are not able to write well. They do not want to practise.
   ______________________________________________
6. Do you want to go on a trek? Do you want to go on a hike?
   ______________________________________________
7. I haven't seen the new Marvel film. I will watch it on Sunday.
   ______________________________________________

## Listening and Speaking

**Form pairs. Each pair will bring to class a picture of something that is used in daily life. The pair will describe how the object in the picture is made, what its components are and how it functions. The pair can also be a bit more creative and draw a picture of their own invention to show in class.**

## Pen it Down

**Write a news report about a young role model from India who has done valuable work in the field of science, especially on sustainability. You can consult the Internet or your school library for information.**

You may use the following points in your report:

- biographical details of this person
- how they became interested in the subject
- what impact they have had on the specific region in India where they work
- how their work has changed their particular field of study
- any awards and recognition that they have received

# 15

# Peter of Haarlem

## Way with Words

### Idioms

**A. Match the idioms related to body parts with their meanings.**

| Idioms | Meanings |
|---|---|
| 1. all ears | a. an earlier start |
| 2. break a leg | b. take care of, watch in order to protect |
| 3. cold feet | c. cry very hard |
| 4. cost an arm and a leg | d. good luck |
| 5. cry your heart out | e. listening attentively |
| 6. give a hand | f. be very expensive |
| 7. head start | g. nervous just before a big event |
| 8. keep an eye on | h. help someone to do something |

**B. Read these idioms related to work and business, and their meanings. Then make sentences of your own using the idioms.**

1. **business as usual**: everything continuing in a normal way, in spite of difficulties

   ______________________________

2. **business before pleasure**: finishing one's work before relaxing and enjoying

   ______________________________

3. **can't stand the pace**: the inability to do things well when there is a lot of pressure

   ______________________________

4. **carve out a niche**: create a place for oneself by means of hard work

   ______________________________

5. **clinch a deal**: reach an agreement on a proposal or an offer

   ______________________________

## Words Used as Nouns and Verbs

**C. Form sentences using the underlined nouns as verbs.**

1. The teacher was writing on the black board.

   ______________________________

2. Only a fool will try to rob this bank.

   ______________________________

3. You will not be allowed to enter the class without your book.

   ______________________________

4. He has set a new world record.

   ______________________________

5. Please pass me the bottle of glue.

   ______________________________

6. This is not the key to this lock.

   ______________________________

7. The pain prevented him from going to the match.

   ______________________________

8. All the rivers have dried up because of this terrible heat.

   ______________________________

9. We will need to get a clock for this room.

   ______________________________

10. We can go for a walk in the park this evening.

    ______________________________

## Grammar in Use

### Reflexive and Indefinite pronouns

You have learnt that pronouns are of different types based on the function they perform in a sentence.

**Reflexive pronouns** refer back to the subject of the sentence. These are **myself, yourself, himself, herself, itself, ourselves, yourselves** and **themselves**.

**Example:** My dog has hurt **itself** while playing.

**Indefinite pronouns** refer to people or things in general, and not someone or something specific. These are **anybody**, **everybody**, **nobody**, **somebody**, **anyone**, **everyone**, **no one**, **someone**, **anything**, **everything**, **nothing** and **something**.

**Example:** **Anyone** could have broken the window.

**A. Complete the sentences with the correct reflexive pronouns.**

1. Can you please help me solve this question? I can't solve it ____________.
2. The driver was tired, so my father decided to drive the car ____________.
3. After seeing ____________ in the mirror, she decided to change her dress.
4. They decorated the Christmas tree ____________.
5. You need to take care of ____________, or else you will fall ill.
6. We can study by ____________ and discuss our doubts tomorrow.

**B. Rewrite these sentences after correcting the errors.**

1. The archeologists searched the site but could not find nothing.

   ________________________________________
2. I have searched anywhere for the keys, but I cannot locate them.

   ________________________________________
3. Would you like everything to eat?

   ________________________________________
4. Anyone informed the police about the robbery.

   ________________________________________
5. She invited everyone for the party but nothing turned up.

   ________________________________________

## Types of Phrases

You have learnt about phrases. There are three types of phrases.

A **noun phrase** functions as a noun in a sentence. It can act as the subject or object. We can identify a noun phrase by asking the question **what**.

**Examples:** **Playing chess** is a good hobby. (What is a good hobby?)
I wish **to become a writer**. (What do you wish?)

An **adjective phrase** does the work of an adjective in a sentence. It modifies a noun or a pronoun.

**Examples:** My friend has **brown eyes**.
The soldiers wore **smart uniforms**.

An **adverb phrase** does the work of an adverb in a sentence. It modifies a verb, an adjective or another adverb. We can identify an adverb phrase by asking the questions **where**, **when** and **how**.

**Examples:** The baby fell **from the cot**. (Where did the baby fall from?)
She made the cake **later in the evening**. (When did she make the cake?)

**C. Underline the phrases in these sentences and state whether they are noun (N), adjective (A) or adverb (AV) phrases.**

1. My brother wants to be an engineer. __________
2. The lady in the pink saree is my mother. __________
3. Did you eat your lunch today? __________

4. My father always drives with care. _________
5. My brother and his friends were disturbing everyone in the house. _________
6. The grapes are of sour taste. _________

## Listening and Speaking

**Form pairs. One person will tell the class of an instance where he/she performed a good deed. The other person will write down the qualities exhibited by the speaker through the good act that he/she did. Once you have written down all the qualities, stand before the class with your partner and talk about him/her.**

## Pen it Down

Imagine that you heard about Peter's brave deeds from one of his neighbours. You were quite impressed with the determination and courage shown by the little boy. When you went back home, you decided to write about Peter, describing his feats of courage.

**Write a second-person account about Peter's act of selflessness, including how you felt when you heard the story, what you would have done in his place and what lessons you have learnt from the story.**

# 16 A Visit from St Nicholas

## Way with Words

### Words Related to Christmas

**A. Match the words with their definitions.**

| A | B |
|---|---|
| 1. reindeer | a. a place where a fire can be lit and the surrounding area on the wall and floor |
| 2. fireplace | b. large deer found in the colder regions of Europe, Asia and Greenland, said to pull Santa's sleigh |
| 3. sleigh | c. something used for beautification |
| 4. decoration | d. a light horse-drawn cart used to carry people over snow and ice |
| 5. present | e. an imaginary bearded old man in a red suit who lives at the North Pole and brings children presents on Christmas Eve |
| 6. Santa Claus | f. something given as a gift |

**B. Match these words and phrases related to Christmas.**

| A | B |
|---|---|
| 1. wrapping | a. Bethlehem |
| 2. Merry | b. paper |
| 3. Christmas | c. pudding |
| 4. plum | d. Christmas |
| 5. Star of | e. carols |

## Grammar in Use

### Demonstrative and Interrogative Pronouns

**Demonstrative pronouns** point out a specific person, place or thing. They are **this, that, these** and **those**.

**Example:** **These** are my books.

**Interrogative pronouns** are used at the beginning of a question. They are **what, which, who, whom** and **whose**.

**Example:** **What** is your name?

**A. Fill in the blanks with the correct pronouns.**

1. __________ is coming for dinner? (Who/Which/What)
2. __________ was a lovely holiday! (What/Which/That)
3. __________ are our fruit trays. (This/These/What)
4. __________ is the school where Sachin Tendulkar studied? (Which/Who/This)
5. __________ gave you this information? (Who/Which/What)
6. __________ is the meaning of this word? (What/Which/That)
7. __________ have you invited as chief guest for the inauguration ceremony? (Whom/Which/What)
8. __________ is our new house. (Whom/Which/That)
9. The people who are vaccinated are safer than __________ who are not vaccinated. (those/these/they)
10. __________ does this cardigan belong to? (Who/Whom/What)

### Subordinating and Correlative Conjunctions

**Correlative conjunctions** are used in pairs to join sentences. They include **both...and, either...or, neither...nor, not only...but also, although...yet** and **whether...or**.

**Example:** His brother speaks **neither** English **nor** Hindi.

**Subordinating conjunctions** are used to join a subordinate clause to an independent clause. They include **although, after, before, because, how, if, once, since, so that, until, unless, when, while, where** and **whether**.

**Example:** **If** you see her, please give her the note.

**B. Complete the sentences using the correct correlative conjunctions from the brackets.**

1. My family plans to shift to Mumbai ________ this year ________ early next year. (but...also/either...or)
2. I like ________ junk food ________ carbonated drinks. (either...or/neither...nor)
3. He is ________ indisciplined ________ rude! (both...and/whether...or)

4. ________ is sports healthy, ________ it ________ helps build friendships and team spirit. (not only...but also/although...yet)

5. I'm yet to decide ________ to have a butterscotch pastry after dinner ________ a chocolate muffin. (either...or/whether...or)

**C. Fill in the blanks with appropriate subordinating conjunctions.**

1. I make it a point to visit my grandparents every weekend ________ I love them dearly.
2. He could make it to the birthday party ________ he was a bit late.
3. ________ you tell the truth, you have nothing to fear.
4. ________ you work hard, you cannot hope to clear this tough competitive exam.
5. I will do the cleaning ________ you do the cooking.

## Listening and Speaking

**Form two groups and think of some questions. Write the answers of these questions on strips of paper. Place the strips in two baskets and give a basket to each group. A student from each group will pick up an answer and the student next to him/her will ask a question to guess the answer. The group that arrives at the correct answer with the fewest number of questions wins.**

## Pen it Down

**A. Imagine you are one of the children in the poem 'A Visit from St Nicholas'. You wake up in the morning to find gifts near the Christmas tree and stockings filled with chocolates. Write a diary entry about your feelings on Christmas Day. Write about what the day means to you, what gifts you got and what you would have liked to say to St Nicholas if you had a chance to meet him.**

________________________________________

________________________________________

________________________________________

________________________________________

________________________________________

________________________________________

________________________________________

________________________________________

________________________________________

B. Imagine that you receive a surprise gift from Santa Claus to travel to any place you would like. You undertake the journey. Write a descriptive account of the place. Discuss what you liked about it, what you did there and what you learned from the visit.

# 17

# In the Rue Bel Tesoro – I

## Comprehension

**Read the passage and answer the questions that follow.**

If the Indian hill stations are to be saved, the Kasauli model needs to be implemented without any delay. Of all the hill stations we have visited, Kasauli was one of the cleanest hill stations, with almost no litter. There was not a single restaurant selling continental and Chinese cuisine, nor did we have to face the pestering of the local guides and touts. And when I say no restaurant, I mean absolutely none. Forget the fancy eateries, we could not even find a bakery one evening when we were in the mood to have some freshly baked cakes. As a result of this, Kasauli retains much of its British era charm and the major contributor to preserving this charm is the army.

The discipline enforced by the army plays a pivotal role in maintaining the beauty of Kasauli. The Sunset Point is the best example of this. Vehicles are strictly prohibited from entering within one kilometre of the Sunset Point. Also, at the actual spot, there are no shops, ice-cream parlours or souvenir pedlars.

If you are to explore Kasauli, there are two main roads that you can take—the Upper Mall Road and the Lower Mall Road. By the side of the roads are bungalows and cottages. If you look from the Lower Mall Road on a clear night, you will be able to see the Shimla lights. For morning and afternoon sunshine, the best place to be is on the Upper Mall Road, which faces both Chandigarh and Shimla. Similar to other cantonment towns in India, there is an old bazaar in Kasauli. We did our only bit of shopping here and bought rock salt and some asafoetida. The woman who sold these was so old that she looked as if she belonged to the period of the Old Testament. If she claimed that she was as old as Methuselah and had been in Kasauli since the time the city was built, we wouldn't have been surprised.

As far as social events are concerned, Kasauli has two major ones. These are held annually and the first one is in the last week of June. It is called Kasauli Week when the army and Kasauli Club organise a number of parties and social gatherings. The grand finale of Kasauli Week is a dance party at the Kasauli Club. The other one is the Founder's Day celebration of The Lawrence School, Sanawar. It takes place in the first week of October, and during that time, the entire town is filled with old Sanwarians.

**A. Choose the correct options to answer the following questions.**

1. Kasauli has much to thank which of the following?
   a. tourist guides ☐ b. army ☐ c. hotels ☐
2. Which of these words is closest in meaning to the word **litter** as used in the passage?
   a. garbage ☐ b. brood ☐ c. spread ☐
3. Why couldn't the writer eat cake in Kasauli?
   a. The writer was not hungry. ☐
   b. The writer did not have time. ☐
   c. There was no bakery in Kasauli. ☐
4. In which month of the year would you be able to attend parties in Kasauli?
   a. October ☐ b. December ☐ c. June ☐
5. If you wanted to see the lights of Shimla, you should be
   a. on the Lower Mall ☐ b. on the Upper Mall ☐ c. in the old bazaar ☐
6. What does the Upper Mall Road face?
   a. both Chandigarh and Shimla ☐
   b. Chandigarh and Dehradun ☐
   c. Chandigarh ☐

**B. Complete the sentences using words from the passage.**

1. There are two ________________ social events in Kasauli.
2. To save the hill stations in India, the Kasauli ________________ should be studied.
3. Like all ________________ towns, Kasauli has a main bazaar.
4. The writer bought ______________ and __________ from the bazaar.
5. No vehicles are allowed near ________________.
6. The grand finale of Kasauli Week is a ________________.

**C. Answer the questions in a few lines.**

1. Why is the town of Kasauli able to retain its old world charm?

   ________________________________________

   ________________________________________

2. Describe what happens during Kasauli Week.

   ________________________________________

   ________________________________________

   ________________________________________

3. How has the army helped in the maintenance of Kasauli as a hill station?

   ________________________________________

   ________________________________________

4. Explain the meaning of the following line in your own words.

   *If she claimed that she was as old as Methuselah and had been in Kasauli since the time the city was built, we wouldn't have been surprised.*

   ________________________________________

   ________________________________________

   ________________________________________

5. Would you like the absence of restaurants and guides at a tourist spot? Give reasons.

   ________________________________________________________________

   ________________________________________________________________

## Way with Words

### Phrasal Verbs

| play off | play along | play around | play at |
|---|---|---|---|
| play back | play down | play on | play out |

**A. Read the meanings and write the correct phrasal verbs with play. Use the help box.**

1. to pretend that something is funny or good just to make someone else happy ____________.
2. to act in a silly manner ____________.
3. to do something just for fun ____________.
4. to listen to something that has been recorded earlier ____________.
5. to try to make something seem less important ____________.
6. a game played to decide the winner of a tie ____________.
7. to use the feelings or fears of another person to one's own advantage ____________.
8. to see something through till the end ____________.

### Feeling Words

**B. Complete the sentences using the correct feeling words from the box.**

| upset | worried | excited | angry | scared | happy | surprised |
|---|---|---|---|---|---|---|

1. It's Abhay's birthday today. He's __________ about his birthday party.
2. Hema was late for school yesterday, and again today. Her teacher is __________.
3. There was a rat in my room. I was so __________!
4. Raman was so __________ with the news, that he threw his phone across the room.
5. My grandparents haven't called since last month. We are __________.
6. I had not been able to study properly for my exam. So, I was pleasantly __________ to find that I had scored well.
7. The sound of birds chirping in the morning makes me ________.

## Grammar in Use

### Direct and Indirect Speech

**Direct speech** includes the exact words of the speaker. The words are placed within quotation marks ('').

**Examples:** The mechanic said, 'The oil in the car engine needs changing.'
'I like chocolate ice cream,' said my friend.

**Indirect speech** reports what someone else said without changing the meaning. The words in indirect speech may differ slightly from the exact words of the speaker. The reporting words **said**, **asked**, **exclaimed** and **requested** are used in indirect speech, along with **that** in place of quotation marks.

**Examples:** The mechanic said that the oil in the car engine needed changing.
My friend said that he likes chocolate ice cream.

**A. Rewrite the sentences in indirect speech.**

1. 'He works very hard,' his father said.

 ______________________________

2. 'We went to London last summer,' Sneha said.

 ______________________________

3. Ram cried, 'Be patient. I'm coming!'

 ______________________________

4. Mother said, 'I was reading the newspaper when he arrived.'

 ______________________________

5. 'I've never been to the fair before,' she said.

 ______________________________

**B. This is an extract from the story *Alice's Adventures in Wonderland.* Change the sentences to indirect speech.**

'Who are YOU?' said the Caterpillar. Alice replied, rather shyly, 'I—I hardly know, sir, just at present—at least I know who I was when I got up this morning, but I think I must have been changed several times since then.'
'What do you mean by that?' said the Caterpillar sternly. 'Explain yourself!'
'I can't explain myself, I'm afraid, sir', said Alice, 'because I'm not myself, you see.'
'I don't see,' said the Caterpillar.
'I'm afraid I can't put it more clearly,' Alice replied very politely, 'for I can't understand it myself to begin with; and being so many different sizes in a day is very confusing.'
'It isn't,' said the Caterpillar.
'Well, perhaps you haven't found it so yet,' said Alice; 'but when you have to turn into a chrysalis—you will some day, you know—and then after that into a butterfly, I should think you'll feel it a little queer, won't you?'

## Listening and Speaking

**Whom/What do you want to be?**

**Each student should tell the class whom/what he/she wants to be for a day. List the things that you would like to do as that person/thing. Speak at least five sentences.**

You may use the following phrases.

- I want to be . . .
- I would start . . .
- I would stop . . .
- I would like to . . .

## Pen it Down

**A. A travelogue is a written or a filmed account of a journey to a particular place. Imagine yourself to be a traveller and write a travelogue. You can write about the place you last visited on a holiday or an imaginary place. Remember to follow these guidelines.**

- Write it in the form of a story told in the first person.
- Include illustrations, photographs and maps.
- Tell the readers about where you stayed, the weather, mode of travelling, and the adventures you had.

**B.** **There has been an influx of refugees in your city. They need help with food and shelter. Write a formal letter to your school principal asking for permission to organise a fundraising drive.**

# 18 In the Rue Bel Tesoro – II

## Way with Words

### Adjectives

**A. Choose the correct adjectives to complete the sentences.**

1. Traffic is __________ now than it used to be earlier.
   a. better ☐ b. more better ☐
2. Ajay is __________ about the competition than I am.
   a. more nervous ☐ b. nervouser ☐
3. I liked the book, although it is a little __________ than the author's previous book.
   a. duller ☐ b. more dull ☐
4. My blue jacket is __________ than the red one.
   a. cleanest ☐ b. cleaner ☐
5. This is the __________ exercise in the book.
   a. tougher ☐ b. toughest ☐
6. Your car is __________ than mine.
   a. faster ☐ b. more faster ☐
7. This palace is __________ than the one we saw yesterday.
   a. more grand ☐ b. grander ☐
8. The view from the top of the hill is __________ than it is from the side of the lake.
   a. more beautiful ☐ b. beautiful ☐
9. The next book in the series is __________ than the last one.
   a. interesting ☐ b. more interesting ☐
10. My new mobile is the __________ of all the ones I have owned.
    a. tinier ☐ b. tiniest ☐

**B. Complete the sentences using farther or further.**

1. How much ________ do we have to walk?
2. I just can't walk any ________.
3. Do you have any ________ questions regarding this project?
4. The hotel is ________ than I had thought!
5. I am enjoying the evening, but the ________ I walk, the ________ behind schedule I get.
6. How much ________ do you wish to take this matter?
7. It's not that much ________ to the railway station.
8. The ________ you go up, the harder the work will be.

## Grammar in Use

### Simple, Compound and Complex Sentences

A **simple sentence** is a basic sentence with a subject and a verb. It has only a main clause.

**Examples:** Shelly played basketball.
The school bus was early.

A **compound sentence** consists of two or more independent clauses joined by coordinating conjunctions.

**Examples:** Sahil studied hard but did not do well in exams.
I was upset for I had lost my watch.

A **complex sentence** consists of an independent clause connected to one or more dependent clauses, using subordinating conjunctions or relative pronouns.

**Examples:** This is the watch which my parents gave me on my graduation.
When I reached the venue, the party was already over.

**Identify the types of sentences by circling the correct options.**

1. My parents go to bed by half past ten.
   a. simple b. compound c. complex
2. I met my friend's cousins today and enjoyed playing with them.
   a. simple b. compound c. complex
3. The big black dog chased the small brown cat.
   a. simple b. compound c. complex
4. Joyce and Ena played football before lunch and then scrabble after lunch.
   a. simple b. compound c. complex
5. On teacher's day, the teachers and the principal went to see the latest release in the new movie theatre.
   a. simple b. compound c. complex

6. The President of the country gave bravery awards to the soldiers who fought bravely in the war.

   a. simple b. compound c. complex

7. The music continued playing for a long time, but the guests had stopped dancing.

   a. simple b. compound c. complex

8. The principal gave a rousing speech on founder's day.

   a. simple b. compound c. complex

9. This house is believed to be haunted.

   a. simple b. compound c. complex

10. She dropped the plate she was holding when her name was announced for the best student award.

   a. simple b. compound c. complex

## Listening and Speaking

**Sit in a circle. In a basket, place paper strips that have the words 'truth' and 'lie' written on them. Play music and circulate the basket. When the music stops, whoever has the basket should pick a strip. If it has 'truth' written on it, the other students can ask him/her a question and he/she has to reply truthfully. If it has 'lie' written on it, the student can tell a lie in response to the question being asked. The rest of the students have to catch the lie spoken by the student. Remember, the other students cannot know what is written on the paper strip!**

## Pen it Down

**Imagine Fran had taken Sasha and Omar with her from the station. Form groups of three and write a short play on this situation. One person can play multiple characters if necessary. The teacher will decide the duration of the play.**

You can include these points in your play.

- The children go home with Fran and live with her till the war ends.
- She helps them find their parents.
- They meet Georgiou and Lena on the way and invite them to come and stay with Fran.
- The children come to know that Fran is their grandmother.
- They meet their father but don't recognise him as he is in disguise.

# Assessment

## Comprehension

**Text A. Read this story about a little boy who lived with his grandparents. Then answer the questions.**

Often, Tom would have some dry bread and watery soup for dinner. Then Tom would go to his grandparents and enjoy story time. Later, he would wish them good night and go to sleep. Tom's four grandparents were each well over ninety. They hardly went out of the room and would just sit huddled in one corner of the bed. Their skins were shrivelled and dry like the skin of an onion. Even in summer, they would be wearing their nightcaps and thick sweaters throughout the day. They hardly had even an ounce of energy left in them. However, all this changed the moment Tom entered their room at night. As soon as the little boy said, 'Good evening' to them, their faces would light up with a happy glow. They would share tales from the time when they were young, which amazed Tom. For that little while, it seemed as if some magic spell had removed the poverty and unhappiness from their home.

### Questions

1. What were the ages of Tom's grandparents? (1 mark)

_______________________________________________

2. How do we know that Tom belonged to a poor family? (2 marks)

_______________________________________________

_______________________________________________

3. What happened after dinner? (2 marks)

_______________________________________________

_______________________________________________

4. Why do you think the grandparents looked forward to Tom's visit? (2 marks)

_______________________________________________

_______________________________________________

5. Describe Tom's grandparents. (3 marks)

_______________________________________________

_______________________________________________

_______________________________________________

6. *'Their skins were shrivelled and dry like the skin of an onion.'*
   a. What does 'shrivelled' mean in this sentence?
   Select and copy **one** correct answer from
   withered    cold    layered    purple-coloured (1 mark)
   b. They hardly had even an ________ of energy left in them.
   Choose and write **one** correct answer from
   atom    iota    once    ounce (1 mark)
7. What message is the writer trying to convey through this passage? (3 marks)

**Text B. Read this passage about how locally grown coloured cotton can provide innovative solutions.**

Colour dyes pollute water and damage the environment, and the production of cotton uses a lot of pesticides. Therefore, the search for fabric that is naturally coloured and can be grown organically has become popular. After over thirty years of research, an Indian variety of coloured cotton will be commercially released by 2022. The Indian Council for Agricultural Research (ICAR) and the All India Coordinated Research Project on Cotton (AICRP) are working on the final trials to test these seeds. Four to five coloured cotton seed varieties are showing promise. Their fibre strength is being tested and locations are being identified where ginning (removing the seeds) and processing can be done. These seeds can also be reused by farmers each year, so wastage will be reduced. In India, 40 local cotton varieties are available in the National Gene Bank of Cotton. These come in various shades of brown and green.

The government has also supported this initiative. On Republic Day, 26 January 2021, an experimental brown cotton range called Kandu was launched in the Indian market to promote naturally coloured cotton.

**Questions**

1. What do coloured dyes do? (2 marks)
2. Which organizations are working on the final trials to test these seeds? (2 marks)
3. After how many years of research would an Indian variety of coloured cotton be commercially released and on which occasion? (2 marks)
5. How many coloured cotton seed varieties are showing promise and what does the testing process involve? (2 marks)
6. In India, how many local cotton varieties are available and where? In which shades do they come? (3 marks)

6. *'...and can be grown organically.'*

   a. What does 'organically' mean in this sentence?
      Select and copy one correct answer from

      naturally organ-based commercially efficiently (1 mark)

   b. These seeds can also be ________ by farmers each year, so wastage will be reduced.
      Choose and write one correct answer from

      crushed destroyed reused sold (1 mark)

7. Which new brand of coloured cotton was launched in India and when? (2 marks)

## NOTES

# NOTES

## NOTES